ONE

The Power of Unity!

"And the glory which You gave Me I have given them, that they may be one just as We are one."
— John 17:22

"Behold, how good and how pleasant it is for brethren to dwell together in unity!"
— Psalm 133:1

...Conversations with God from the journals of...

NATHAN A. FRENCH

ONE: *The Power of Unity!*

Copyright © 2021 by Nathan A. French

Published by Aviva Publishing
Lake Placid, NY
518-523-1320
www.avivapubs.com

All rights reserved. No part of this book may be reproduced or transmitted in any form or by any means without the written permission of the author. For inquiries, contact:

Nathan French
info@rockrevivalcenter.com

Scripture taken from the New King James Version (NKJV). Copyright © 1982 by Thomas Nelson, Inc. Used by permission. All rights reserved.

Scripture quotations marked KJV are taken from the King James Version of the Holy Bible and are in the Public Domain.

Scripture quotations taken from The Holy Bible, New International Version® NIV® Copyright © 1973 1978 1984 2011 by Biblica, Inc.TM Used by permission. All rights reserved worldwide.

ISBN: 978-1-63618-109-7

ISBN: 978-1-63618-110-3, eBook

Library of Congress Control Number: 2021911667

Editor: Tyler Tichelaar, Superior Book Productions

Cover Design & Interior Layout: Larry Alexander, Superior Book Productions

First Edition

Printed in the United States of America

Dedication

To God the Father, my Savior Jesus Christ, and the Holy Spirit
—the great three in one—
who chose to give birth to this continuing work entrusted to me
by that still small voice that has gently beckoned me to "Come sit."
These words have been a gift to me, so I eagerly share them with you.

Acknowledgments

To my wife, Danielle—what would I do without her—and my daughters, for the inspiration and love they bless me with.

To my dad, Gene French, my passionate father, who places my interests above his own and who has been an excellent example of Christlikeness through grace and love.

To my mom, Betty French, for believing in the validity of God's words spoken to me; for cheering me on to be the man God intended me to be; and for overseeing the publishing of this book.

To the *Rock Revival Center* family, who have joined us in this journey and have determined to love God by loving people!

To all intercessors and ministry partners who have understood the vision God has given us and have diligently prayed and given of their resources that His will be done on earth as it is in heaven.

To the many fellow pastors, evangelists, revivalists, prophets, teachers, and apostles I've met and learned from. To those who have opened doors for ministry, I thank you. It is my honor to serve Christ with you.

To you, the reader. May you be filled by the *water* of the Holy Spirit as you read *ONE: The Power of Unity!*.

Contents

Foreword	13
Introduction	15
Nathan's Story (Testimony)	17
A Clarification	21
MAY 2012	23
• **May 1:** Dependence	25
• **May 3:** Instruction; Will You?	26
• **May 5:** Healing Explosion; Why Limit Me?; Paradise of Obedience; Receive What I Have to Give; Delight in My Plan; Today	28
• **May 9:** A Word to a Man: You Are My Creation; Your Future; It Is Finished; Your Daughter; Let Me Heal Your Heart; Romans 8	33
• **May 12:** Mothers: A Giver of Life; Remembrance; Show Appreciation	40
• **May 20:** Amazing Grace; Grace Poured Out; Grace Deserved; Under the Law; Old Covenant; Experience Grace	42
• **May 23:** Justified; Deceived; The Cross—a Finished Work or Not; Faith Without Works; Sin No More; Grace Builds My Church; Evidence of Faith; Paid in Advance	47
• **May 25:** I AM; Serve with Joy; Selfish Serving	52
• **May 27:** Washing Feet; Motivated by Pride; Motivated by Obedience	54

JUNE 2012 — 57

- **June 1:** Contentment; Discontentment — 59
- **June 6:** Hearing My Voice (Instructions for Equipping Meeting); Steps to Hearing; Practicums — 60
- **June 7:** You Are My Student — 62
- **June 9:** The Moving of My Spirit; Check Yourself — 63
- **June 10:** Let Go of Sickness; Rise Up, Church — 65
- **June 11:** An Intimate Exhortation — 68
- **June 12:** Proverbs (Definition: a short pithy saying) — 70
- **June 15:** Lift the Name of Jesus; Speak to the People — 72
- **June 16:** Tend Your Garden — 75
- **June 17:** The Covenant of Grace Prayer — 76
- **June 18:** Let Me; Money Is a Tool — 77
- **June 20:** Sheep and Wolves — 78
- **June 22:** More About Grace — 79
- **June 23:** Hearing My Voice; Practice Hearing; Steps to Hearing; Questions You Might Ask; Do Not Be Afraid; Ear Blockers — 81
- **June 30:** Sheep vs. Wolves; Maturity; Priorities; Dead Branches, 1 Timothy 4 — 85

JULY 2012 — 89

- **July 6:** Wisdom Whispers from Heaven — 91
- **July 9:** A Touch — 92
- **July 11:** A Journey; Focus on the Prize; Colors of Freedom; A Lifeline; Lessons; Things to Consider; Large Ships — 93
- **July 12:** Launch Pad; The Righteous Will Shine; One Attribute Results in Another; Deeds and Titles; It's *NOT* Meant to Be a Secret — 98
- **July 13:** Children of the Living God (a Song); Thunder; Weakness vs. Strength; I Am Your Weapon; Revelation; Wayward Thinkers; Greed; Nuggets of Truth…; A Song — 101
- **July 13:** Heaven's Touch; Allow My Spirit to Come; Heaven's Portion Cannot Be Contained — 106

- **July 14:** Concerns — 108
- **July 15:** Independence from Dependence — 109
- **July 16:** Building a Church — 111
- **July 18:** How to Give Me Your Whole Heart; You Are…; I AM the Holy Spirit; Hope, Faith, Love — 112
- **July 19:** I Am a Developer; Be an Overcomer; Send the Angels; Let It Be Known; Lavish Love — 115
- **July 22:** Some Things Worth Mentioning; I Write Through Your Pen; I Have Heard — 119
- **July 24:** Represent Me Well — 122
- **July 25:** Life of a Chicken; Why — 123
- **July 27:** A Note on Prophesy; A Paradise Glimpse; A Trip to Heaven — 125
- **July 28:** Build My Church; Preparing a Worship Service — 131
- **July 29:** The Ultimate Treasure — 134

AUGUST 2012 — 137

- **August 4:** Listen to Me!; Yeah; Run the Race; Suffering for a Season; Seek to Be Approved; Revival Is Here; My Name Is Jesus — 139
- **August 6:** I Make All Things New; Occupy the Land; Nothing Is Impossible; Watch For…; You Cannot Save Yourselves; Fill Up; A Breaking Dam; Do Great Exploits — 144
- **August 11:** My Agenda/God's Agenda—Miracles and Healings — 149
- **August 12:** Instructions for My People — 151
- **August 14:** Teen Challenge — 153
- **August 17:** A House Upon the Rock — 155
- **August 19:** Green Pastures — 157
- **August 21:** Willpower; Hearing Correctly — 159
- **August 23:** Oil of Gladness — 161
- **August 25:** The Mission; Guidance; Discipline Yourself; Love Others as Yourself; Discouragement: A Sidetrack to the Mission; The Great Commission — 162
- **August 26:** Arizona — 166

ONE: The Power of Unity

- **August 29:** Wisdom of Heaven; Our Book; A Story — 169
- **August 30:** Victory; Overcoming Leads to Victory; Victory Produced Through Testing and Training; Land of Failure; Stones of Victory — 172
- **August 31:** Observing the Day of Rest; Religious Pride — 175

SEPTEMBER 2012 — 177
- **September 1:** Refusing to Eat; Come — 179
- **September 2:** Come to Me in the Quiet; Overcome the Devil — 181
- **September 4:** Assignments from Heaven; Favor; A Mission; I Am; Be Who I Have Said You Are; I Am Your Friend — 184
- **September 13:** Run the Race; Whose Plans?; Whose Will?; What Can I Do?; Lift Up the Son; You Are My Inheritance — 189
- **September 14:** A Garden — 193
- **September 15:** Imprisoned — 194
- **September 18:** Stay on My Path — 195
- **September 19:** Teach Victory — 197
- **September 20:** Word to a Christian Leader: My Beloved; You Will Prophesy; A Voice to the Nations; Fill up Again; Bring Two Cultures Together; Come — 198
- **September 22:** El Shaddai — 202
- **September 24:** Things to Remember; A New Song — 203
- **September 25:** My Goodness Alone; Transition; A Broad Perspective; My Words are Simple; Serving Others Brings Joy — 205
- **September 27:** Prepare for the Harvest; Words to Ponder — 208
- **September 29:** Message for a Young Woman — 210

OCTOBER 2012 — 213
- **October 10:** New Direction; Don't Open the Door to the Stranger; Be Single-Minded — 215

- **October 12:** The Law: Keep My Laws; Misuse of Spiritual Gifts; Blocked Ears; Empowered Living; The Truth About Keeping the Law; Image; Abundance — 217
- **October 13:** A Journey — 223
- **October 15:** To a Worship Leader: I AM; The Best Soil — 225
- **October 17:** An Assignment; Maturity Is Not Easy — 228
- **October 21:** The Heart: The Heart Matters; Good and Evil; A Hardened Heart; Fresh Bread; Birthright; Action Is Proof — 230
- **October 21:** It's NOT About — 234
- **October 22:** Finances: Money Is a Tool; Crack Down on Your Money; Discipline Is Part of Discipleship; Wants vs. Needs — 236
- **October 23:** An Open Rebuke — 238
- **October 24:** Rest in Your Work — 239
- **October 25:** The Sweet Spot — 240
- **October 26:** A Tip; I Still Discipline Those I Love; A Gift of Service; Self-Reliance or God-Dependence — 241
- **October 27:** A Move of My Spirit — 243
- **October 28:** To My Praying Children — 245

NOVEMBER 2012 — 247
- **November 1:** Living Water; Abundant Life; Correction; Will You? — 249
- **November 2:** A Mighty Army; Child Likeness; A Rhyme with a Message — 251
- **November 9:** Intimacy, Part 1: God's Sons; Share the Secrets; Time; Fear of Intimacy; Made Worthy; A Snare; A Protection; Love and Obedience; Where Is Your Treasure?; I Desire Intimacy — 254
- **November 10:** Intimacy, Part 2: Seek Me; Drive Out Rebellion; Reward of Intimacy — 260
- **November 18:** Faith: Faith Fed by Action; Breakthrough; If You Do; Practice Obedience; The Greatest Is Love; Faith Dulled by Fear; Fill Up on Faith — 262

- **November 21:** Pace Yourself; Full Surrender — 267
- **November 23:** Building a Church: A Family; Elements of Success; Make Strong Leaders; Breathe; Infrastructure — 269
- **November 24:** My Church: The Foundation; Unstable Ground; Great Leaders; Broaden Your Horizons; Self-Check — 272
- **November 30:** Evangelism: Purification; Refinement; Gold; Rebellion; The Harvest; The Bread of Life — 275

DECEMBER 2012 — 279
- **December 5:** Fantasy vs. Reality: Reality; Fantasy; The Christmas Tree; One; Seek Wisdom — 281
- **December 14:** Christmas: eration of the Cross; Faith; Love; Joy; Religious Pride; A Baby Born to Die; Lord of All; Faith in Action — 285

Appendix — 291
- **Testimony:** Watches — 293
- **Testimony:** Metal Dissolved — 295
- **Testimony:** My First Boat — 297
- **Testimony:** Another Boat — 299
- **Testimony:** The Suburban and the Audi — 302
- **Testimony:** Introduction to President Trump — 304

Addendum — 309
- How to Hear My Voice — 311
- A Prayer to Receive Christ — 313
- A Prayer of Release — 314
- A Prayer of Forgiveness of Self — 315

About the Author — 317
Speaker Page — 319
Also by Nathan French — 321

Foreword

ONE: The Power of Unity! is a continuation of journal entries written during my conversations with the Lord from May 2012 through December 2012 and is a sequel to *It's NOT Meant to Be a Secret* and *Rushing the Flood Gates of Heaven*. Hearing your accounts of how you have learned to hear His voice gives me great joy. So it is with eagerness that I share more with you.

Introduction

It is an honor to share this life-changing content with you. My hope has been to build up and encourage all who will listen. As you read *ONE: The Power of Unity!*, remember that unity is the mindset of the Kingdom of Heaven.

You have been chosen for a specific time in history to gain wisdom and understanding to change the world around you. Spending quiet time with the creator, Himself, is my most valuable treasure, and I hope it will become the same for you.

The Lord is so good, and His plans are to prosper you in all you do, according to His will and purpose.

> *"For I know the plans I have for you,' declares the Lord, 'plans to prosper you and not to harm you, plans to give you hope and a future.'" (Jeremiah 29:11 NIV)*

This great adventure is one thing I am so glad I did not miss out on. As you read, remember that before Jesus went to the cross, He cried out to His Father:

> *"I do not pray for these alone, but also for those who will believe in Me through their word; that they all may be one, as You, Father, are in Me, and I in You; that they also may be one in Us, that the world may believe that You sent Me." (John 17:20-21 NKJV)*

The Word of God instructs His people to keep the unity of the Spirit. The Apostle Paul says it this way:

> "I, therefore, the prisoner of the Lord, beseech you to walk worthy of the calling with which you were called, with all lowliness and gentleness, with longsuffering, bearing with one another in love, endeavoring to keep the unity of the Spirit in the bond of peace." (Ephesians 4:1-3 NKJV)

You will be exceedingly empowered as you read and accept this inspired revelation and learn more and more how to fully adopt the ways of His Kingdom. There is but ONE God. The Lord our God is ONE!

> "For there is one God and ONE Mediator between God and men, the Man Christ Jesus." (1 Timothy 2:5 NKJV)

> "Jesus answered him, 'The first of all the commandments is: "Hear, O Israel, the Lord our God, the Lord is ONE."'" (Mark 12:29 NKJV)

Nathan's Story
(Testimony)

As a young man, I was not walking with the Lord, even though I had accepted Him when I was about seven. I was spending most of my time rebelling against almost everything I had been taught that was right. I got tired of my dad—a pastor—and the rest of my family telling me what to do. I decided to move from my home in Washington State to the sunny beach-filled state of Florida. While there, I did a lot of drugs, had a lot of sex, and I burned through a lot of money...but it was never enough. My life was one big, ongoing party. I thought that doing whatever I wanted, whenever I wanted, was real freedom. I was so very wrong! No one stood a chance at telling me what to do because I was far too self-centered and prideful to listen. It got to the point where I was smoking pot just about every day. I experimented with cocaine and ecstasy, and I drank enough alcohol to kill a rhino. The more I gave my life over to sin, the more lost and empty I became.

One day, I woke up in a very strange place—the psych ward of a Florida hospital. As I looked around, everyone was a stranger. When I asked why I was there and how I got there, no one would tell me. I was extremely sad and lonely. Soon a familiar face entered the room—I began to cry as I looked up into the eyes of my father. He said, "Son, do you know what day it is?" I said, "No, Dad, I don't." He said, "It's your birthday! The devil tried to take your life, but the Lord intervened, and I've come to take you home."

I had attempted suicide. The seed had been planted when I watched the film *The Client*. In the beginning of the movie, a high-roller attorney decides to commit suicide before a mob hitman can kill him. He drives down an old lonely road, hooks himself up to the exhaust pipe of his car, and commits suicide by inhaling the fumes. It looked like such an easy way out. Subconsciously, I began to process suicide as a way out of my messed-up life. I wrote a suicide note, addressed to everyone who cared about me, apologizing for any pain it would cause them. I gathered up a vacuum hose and some big garbage bags and drove until I found a road like the one in the movie. Then I hooked myself up to the exhaust pipe and inhaled carbon monoxide until I passed out cold.

Seconds from death, my van ran out of gas, stopping the flow of deadly gas to my lungs. It wasn't long before I came to and found myself lying face down on the floor against the melted plastic of the vacuum hose, which had seared the fingers on my left hand to the bone. My mind was blown, so I began to wander aimlessly around on foot until I came to a convenience store parking lot. A clerk noticed me and, realizing something was very wrong, called 911. I was picked up and taken to the local hospital where the doctors discovered a life-threatening amount of carbon monoxide in my bloodstream. I was treated and taken to a psych ward—that strange place I mentioned earlier for people who try to harm themselves. The mental diagnosis was schizophrenia, but my parents would not allow the prescribed remedy of drugs for what they knew was a spiritual problem.

My father met me right where I was—all messed up and broken. I will never forget seeing his face that day—the sadness and anguish. My earthly father became an extension of my heavenly father. After a week of convalescing, my dad drove me and my van across the country, stopping at hospitals along the way so my blisters could be opened and the infection could be scrubbed away.

Finally, we were home, but I was in excruciating pain for months as I underwent extensive skin grafting and rehabilitation. Skin was taken from my left leg to rebuild my fingers. Doctors and specialists said I would never again be able to drive a car or function normally in society. To make matters worse, I had no short-term memory, so I would ask the same questions over and over again, exhausting whoever had the patience to be around me. My medical bills were well over $100,000, and the pain of my reality did not end there—but it was a turning point for me. Later, the hospital decided to write off my bill as charity—this kindness reminded me of God's forgiveness.

Repentance literally means, "To turn around or change direction." I had reached brokenness. Like a wild horse, I could be no good to my master until I was broken. I began to turn my life back to the Lord. I received all kinds of prayers, and the Lord began healing my mind, rebuilding it with the truth in His Word. I memorized Scripture and a message from Pastor John Hagee titled, "Battle Cry." I now have a new attitude of gratitude!

With the same hand that was burned and wounded, I've written over 100 Christian songs, and today I am not the same man I was. This experience has refined me like gold under fire. I know I'm still far from pure, but I am allowing the process to continue. There is not a day that goes by that I'm not thankful the Lord allowed this horrible experience into my life. I chose the wrong path, and God allowed me to suffer the consequences, but in the end, the Lord has used my brokenness for good. If I had known the difficulties my rebellion would cause, I would have followed Christ and done what was right from the beginning.

Five years later, during the same week as my attempted suicide, Danielle became my wife. What a gift God has given to me. The

Lord has blessed us with two amazing daughters. I'm starting to see the rewards of a surrendered life to Christ: Peace—love—joy. Now that's real freedom! I know it's only the beginning of what He wants to do in me, and I know He wants to do the same for you—replace your rebellion with His peace. Are you willing? My dad always said, "A wise man learns from his own mistakes, and a wiser man learns from the mistakes of others, but a fool from neither." God has placed a special purpose in each one of us, and the good news is that He likes to finish what He starts!

Note: If you are reading this testimony and you have a son or daughter who has decided to try the delights of sin for a season, pray for him or her. I know my mom and dad never stopped praying for me, even when things seemed hopeless. There is power in prayer!

A Clarification

You are about to experience the reveal of my private journal—selected entries of God's spoken words to me, listed by date in chronological order. Because the Godhead is doing most of the speaking, regular text is used for ease of reading. Anything in *italics* are my own words, except for the Scriptures, which have references following them.

May 2012

May 1

Dependence

I went before you and set up your way. I placed prizes and challenges along the path. Rewards and riddles are waiting as I lead you on this path of dependence.

This government's plan is to create dependence on itself, which is idolatry and breaks My command of having no other gods before Me.

> *"You shall have no other gods before Me." (Exodus 20:3 NKJV)*

I will bring My righteous judgment to tear down the idols of man.

Each section of time has been perfectly allotted. Each standard of measure has been calculated in advance to be maximized by its purpose. Put your foot in the water, beloved. Speak to the rock. Silence the voice of the naysayer. You will succeed.

There will always be some wolves around you, but they cannot break through My protection. They will rather strengthen My defenses in you. Fighting wolves will cause you to be strong and bold for My purposes. You will weep tears of joy and not one tear will be wasted for I will match them one for one as the healing continues. This is the time. This is the place for encounters. Just like the days of old, I am not decreasing. You are not a sinner saved by grace but a saint saved by grace ever flowing.

May 3

Here I am, Lord, awaiting your instruction.

Instruction

I will purge everything to bring life. I will recall every reward that was taken by the fowler.

> *"Our soul has escaped as a bird from the snare of the fowlers; the snare is broken, and we have escaped." (Psalm 124:7 NKJV)*

I will express My life through you and more will be given. Remember Me when you prosper. Do not forget the dependence you have learned. When My book, *It's* NOT *Meant to Be a Secret*, crosses the seas, keep yourself grounded in My heart of love. Lean on Me for your rest. Lend a hand toward the weak that they will be made strong. Give to Me according to your faith. Travel My rivers as they guide you toward My mouth. My words travel as fish looking to return to their birthplace to lay their eggs, guided by My design. How do the fish know their origination point? The right combination of smells confirms their starting point and they return to be duplicators of life.

Does a tree know where it is planted? Certainly not. But the planter knows its placement because he put it in the ground. Your roots go deep down into My heart because you were willing to be planted in the fertile soil. A surfer who rides the wind is at the mercy of it, but he who builds upon the Rock is not blown by chance. I am deleting your desperation and giving you distinction that brings kingdom definition.

Will You?

Will you go to the Barn House?

Will you work My land?

Will you go to the office and write with My hand?

Will you fly across the ocean while heaven is here?

Will you sing like the songbird while people draw near?

Will you plan the adventure as I lead every stage?

Will you guide My people from the storms that still rage?

Know My design and design what I show

For all will be cherished, when I send you, you'll go.

Peace is a breath—like a changing of wind,

Like a blanket I give you, to blot out the sin.

May 5

Healing Explosion

Welcome to My healing explosion, says the Lord God Almighty. I have come to free the slaves of demonic oppression and to shake the foundations of all that is wicked—to bring forth a revolution of all that is righteous. Your faces will shine forth as the sun in the Kingdom of your Father, who is the first and the last, the beginning and the end, the alpha and the omega, who has not, nor ever will, lose His power and authority from heaven toward earth, even now and certainly forever more.

> *"Then the righteous will shine forth as the sun in the Kingdom of their Father. He who has ears to hear, let him hear!"* (Matthew 13:43 NKJV)

Why Limit Me?

Do you, My children, know that I am endless? Why then do you limit Me in your thoughts? Throw off your unbelief and cast aside all your evil ways and I will show you what you have never seen—an outpouring of My Spirit that crushes the shackles from every captive.

> *"Beware, brethren, lest there be in any of you an evil heart of unbelief in departing from the living God." (Hebrews 3:12 NKJV)*

Who will hold hands out before Me in surrender? Now I shower you with new faith that sanctifies the very ground beneath your feet and redeems the reward of life from all forms of deadness.

Paradise of Obedience

Does your sin satisfy? Walk from the ashes, My people. Step into the paradise of obedience to your God so that you will finally enter My rest with the outpouring of joy unspeakable and the prosperity of your souls.

> *"For we who have believed do enter that rest." (Hebrews 4:3 NKJV)*

I bring the miracles of your renewed bodies. I will heal every root of bitterness as you learn to forgive, if only you release yourselves of the walls that have imprisoned your hearts. I will bring back the playfulness of the child in you as you walk by faith and not by sight alone.

> *"Pursue peace with all people, and holiness, without which no one will see the Lord: looking carefully lest anyone fall short of the grace of God; lest any root of bitterness springing up cause trouble and by this many become defiled." (Hebrews 12:14-15 NKJV)*

Do you not know that you are priceless? Do you not know how much you are loved? I love you with the purity of heaven and long that you will find satisfaction in Me alone, your creator whom you have in many ways denied. Who would reject life and chase after what is dead without first being deceived? Walk now in the light and I will heal your land.

> *"But if we walk in the light as He is in the light, we have fellowship with one another, and the blood of Jesus Christ His Son cleanses us from all sin." (1 John 1:7 NKJV)*

Anything that is not from faith is sin.

> *"Do you have faith? Have it to yourself before God. Happy is he who does not condemn himself in what he approves. But he who doubts is condemned if he eats, because he does not eat from faith; for whatever is not from faith is sin." (Romans 14:22-23 NKJV)*

Repent of your unbelief and surely I will forgive you and cleanse you from all unrighteousness that there will be joy in My house and love that cannot be contained.

> *"Now He did not do many mighty works there because of their unbelief." (Matthew 13:58 NKJV)*

> *"Immediately the father of the child cried out and said with tears, 'Lord, I believe; help my unbelief!'" (Mark 9:24 NKJV)*

Receive What I Have to Give

Where My presence abides, there is freedom. Where My heaven pours out, there is oneness—perfect unity and harmony of heart. Remember My promises; each one will be kept. If I say it, it will come to pass. Rise up in Spirit and truth and receive all that I have to give. You must know by now, My people, that I, the Lord your God, have come to challenge your faith that it will be made strong so that you will be prepared for greatness. Grow in strength and sing out from the joy of understanding so that you can enter My rest. My peace is a result of patience. My love should be as an explosion of the expression of glory you were meant to take part in.

Delight in My Plan

To share in My glory, you first must share in My suffering, which is nothing compared to the pleasant purpose I have made for you to enjoy. Delight in My plan, for it is good. Learn and grow in understanding from wisdom that it may be applied, then applauded, by the angels I've called to go with you. Your souls will burst with life as you give Me more time and we grow in intimacy. I know some of you fear time alone with Me because of your wicked deeds, but remember I am a loving God, full of grace and mercy.

> *"Let us therefore come boldly to the throne of grace that we may obtain mercy and find grace to help in time of need." (Hebrews 4:16 NKJV)*

I am calling out to you through the darkness, and I am asking you to step into the light, once and for all, so you will be free, as I Myself am free. I paid the ransom for your freedom yet many still remain under the heaviness of their past sins.

> *"And this is the condemnation, that the light has come into the world, and men loved darkness rather than light, because their deeds were evil." (John 3:19 NKJV)*

Today

Today is your day of salvation. Today is your day to lay down your hopelessness and despair. Today—at this very moment—is the time to give Me the wheel so I can steer you from the cliff of destruction to the safety of My wings of refuge.

> *"For He says: 'In an acceptable time I have heard you, and in the day of salvation I have helped you.' Behold, now is the accepted time; behold, now is the day of salvation." (2 Corinthians 6:2 NKJV)*

I will surround your sorrows and end your loneliness. As you step toward Me, you will see My divine design. Being healed is a choice of your own will. Some do not want to be healed for fear of losing the attention it brings. Some cannot see beyond the wall of unbelief. Today, I will give you reason to believe that you too may receive all you have hoped for from faith as I, your God, deliver the substance of My design to make all things new, even to raise the dead to life.

> *"Now faith is the substance of things hoped for, the evidence of things not seen." (Hebrews 11:1 NKJV)*

May 9 – A Word to a Man

You Are My Creation

You are My creation and I am pleased with what I have knitted together in your mother's womb.

> *"For you formed my inward parts; you covered me in my mother's womb." (Psalm 139:13 NKJV)*

I can see your troubles and I know your pains and fears. I tell you the truth—you are not condemned. Romans, chapter 8[1] is My letter to you, reminding you of My grace and great love. I accept you just the way you are and I am pleased with you, beloved.

Remember when you were just a boy and you sat in your room and wondered if I was real? I was there! Yes, it is I, the Lord God Almighty, the winner of your soul. Do you not know that I wish to lavish you with every good and perfect thing?

> *"Every good gift and every perfect gift is from above, and comes down from the Father of lights, with whom there is no variation or shadow of turning." (James 1:17 NKJV)*

---

1 The text of Romans 8 appears at the end of this chapter for easy reference.

Your Future

Do not worry about your future; it is in the palm of My hand. Your physical body is an expression of your spiritual condition. I have come to give you life and abundance in every way.

> *"I have come that they may have life, and that they may have it more abundantly." (John 10:10 NKJV)*

Don't be so hard on yourself. Be gracious. Know Me and you will know the truth.

> *"Jesus said to him, 'I am the way, the truth, and the life. No one comes to the Father except through Me.'" (John 14:1 NKJV)*

Those who hold themselves under the law cannot be free.

> *"But if you are led by the Spirit, you are not under the law." (Galatians 5:18 NKJV)*

I smile when I see you get up in the morning, knowing that the victory over your life is already won.

> *"But thanks be to God, who gives us the victory through our Lord Jesus Christ." (1 Corinthians 15:67 NKJV)*

I will bring joy back into your home and will breathe on your flame so all will know that I live.

It Is Finished

Remember, it's not what you can do for Me, your God—it's what has already been done for you. "It is finished," means you have not become just a sinner saved by grace but a saint saved by grace. You are a son—NOT an outsider. I welcome you into My royal priesthood!

> *"But you are a chosen generation, a royal priesthood, a holy nation, His own special people, that you may proclaim the*

> *praises of Him who called you out of darkness into His marvelous light." (1 Peter 2:9 NKJV)*

There is still a place at My table. You have not been given a death sentence but a call to renewed life! Will you come, beloved? Will you lay down all that does not agree with My truth? Will you seek after Me with diligence as I reward your every effort? There is a way that seems right to a man, but in the end, it leads only to deadness.

> *"There is a way that seems right to a man, but its end is the way of death." (Proverbs 16:25 NKJV)*

The way that seems right is the process of figuring things out with a brilliant mind. My Spirit of Truth bypasses the mind and sends a message to the light-filled places of the heart. I will shine in the depths of your wounded soul and your garden will burst with outrageous love and radical faith. Everything you give to Me will be restored, and then given back to you. I love you with the fullness of the heavens and have told you that nothing is impossible as you put your trust in Me.

> *"But Jesus looked at them and said, 'With men it is impossible, but not with God; for with God all things are possible.'" (Mark 10:27 NKJV)*

Your Daughter

Your daughter is in My hands. Can you trust her to Me, her designer?

Let Me Heal Your Heart

Will you let Me restore all forms of brokenness? Let Me out of the box, My brilliant friend—I am bigger than what you perceive. What I have planned for you is endless and it's not too late.

Acknowledge Me in all that you do and I will guide your every step down the straight path that leads to life.

> *"He restores my soul; He leads me in the paths of righteousness for His name's sake." (Psalm 23:3 NKJV)*

Be My hands and feet to this lost and broken world. Shine before men that they will know I live.

> *"Let your light so shine before men, that they may see your good works and glorify your Father in heaven." (Matthew 5:16 NKJV)*

Settle your heart before Me and let Me heal your land.

> *"If My people who are called by My name will humble themselves, and pray and seek My face, and turn from their wicked ways, then I will hear from heaven, and will forgive their sin and heal their land." (2 Chronicles 7:14 NKJV)*

Return to Me, My child, and I will return to you. Walk in renewal and enter My rest; then work from there, consumed by My peace.

> *"Take My yoke upon you and learn from me, for I am gentle and lowly in heart, and you will find rest for your souls." (Matthew 11:29 NKJV)*

I am healing your heart.

Romans 8 (NKJV)

Free from Indwelling Sin

There is therefore now no condemnation to those who are in Christ Jesus, who do not walk according to the flesh, but according to the Spirit. For the law of the Spirit of life in Christ Jesus has made me free from the law of sin and death. For what the law could not do in that it was weak through the flesh, God did by sending His own Son in the likeness of sinful flesh, on account of sin: He condemned sin in the flesh, that the righteous requirement of the law might be fulfilled in us who do not walk according to the flesh but according to the Spirit. For those who live according to the flesh set their minds on the things of the flesh, but those who live according to the Spirit, the things of the Spirit. For to be carnally minded is death, but to be spiritually minded is life and peace. Because the carnal mind is enmity against God; for it is not subject to the law of God, nor indeed can be. So then, those who are in the flesh cannot please God.

But you are not in the flesh but in the Spirit, if indeed the Spirit of God dwells in you. Now if anyone does not have the Spirit of Christ, he is not His. And if Christ is in you, the body is dead because of sin, but the Spirit is life because of righteousness. But if the Spirit of Him who raised Jesus from the dead dwells in you, He who raised Christ from the dead will also give life to your mortal bodies through His Spirit who dwells in you.

Sonship Through the Spirit

Therefore, brethren, we are debtors—not to the flesh, to live according to the flesh. For if you live according to the flesh you will die; but if by the Spirit you put to death the deeds of the body, you will live. For as many as are led by the Spirit of God, these are sons of God. For you did not receive the spirit of bondage again to fear, but you received the Spirit of adoption by whom we cry out, "Abba, Father." The Spirit Himself bears witness with our spirit that we are children of God, and if children, then heirs—heirs of God and joint heirs with Christ, if indeed we suffer with Him, that we may also be glorified together.

From Suffering to Glory

For I consider that the sufferings of this present time are not worthy to be compared with the glory which shall be revealed in us. For the earnest expectation of the creation eagerly waits for the revealing of the sons of God. For the creation was subjected to futility, not willingly, but because of Him who subjected it in hope; because the creation itself also will be delivered from the bondage of corruption into the glorious liberty of the children of God. For we know that the whole creation groans and labors with birth pangs together until now. Not only that, but we also who have the first fruits of the Spirit, even we ourselves groan within ourselves, eagerly waiting for the adoption, the redemption of our body. For we were saved in this hope, but hope that is seen is not hope; for why does one still hope for what he sees? But if we hope for what we do not see, we eagerly wait for it with perseverance.

Likewise the Spirit also helps in our weaknesses. For we do not know what we should pray for as we ought, but the Spirit Himself makes intercession for us with groaning which cannot be uttered. Now He who searches the hearts knows what the mind of the Spirit is, because He makes intercession for the saints according to the will of God.

And we know that all things work together for good to those who love God, to those who are the called according to His purpose. For whom He foreknew, He also predestined to be conformed to the image of His Son, that He might be the firstborn among many brethren. Moreover whom He predestined, these He also called; whom He called, these He also justified; and whom He justified, these He also glorified.

God's Everlasting Love

What then shall we say to these things? If God is for us, who can be against us? He who did not spare His own Son, but delivered Him up for us all, how shall He not with Him also freely give us all things? Who shall bring a charge against God's elect? It is God who justifies. Who is he who condemns? It is Christ who died, and furthermore is also risen, who is even at the right hand of God, who also makes intercession for us. Who shall separate us from the love of Christ? Shall tribulation, or distress, or persecution, or famine, or nakedness, or peril, or sword? As it is written:

"For Your sake we are killed all day long; We are accounted as sheep for the slaughter."

Yet in all these things we are more than conquerors through Him who loved us. For I am persuaded that neither death nor life, nor angels nor principalities nor powers, nor things present nor things to come, nor height nor depth, nor any other created thing, shall be able to separate us from the love of God which is in Christ Jesus our Lord."

May 12 – Mothers

A Giver of Life

Where would we be without mothers? Would anyone be born? I sent My son, Jesus, to be born from a mother who was selected for her rare purity. In the same way, I have selected you—the mothers here—according to yours. Each of you will also give birth to what is from the Spirit. Any mother knows that it's not easy to give birth. Any mother knows what it is like to hand your heart away and be afraid that it may not live. To be a giver of life is a very important role that is only the beginning of a very long and challenging process. Daughters, you are precious duplicators of the Kingdom of God. My royal blood flows through your veins and you are connected to a beautiful supply of what will never stop producing—the life that pours from heaven.

Remembrance

Thank you, beloved mothers, for your faithful service to My Kingdom, for I have collected all forms of kindness in My remembrance. Remember when your heart was in your hands and you had to say goodbye to your child and release them into My hands? I was there to receive your gift. In every act of selflessness, service, and sacrifice—even when it was just to hand over a

Kleenex, I was there. I cherish you, My mighty mothers, because you were beautifully made to do certain things extraordinarily well. I applaud you this day and every day on for your endless service to your King, for as you have served them, you have served Me, your God. "He that is greatest among you will be slave of all," shows that each one must learn from the example of their mother's service.

> *"But he who is greatest among you shall be your servant. And whoever exalts himself will be humbled, and he who humbles himself will be exalted." (Matthew 23:11-12 NKJV)*

Mothers must also learn from their daughters. Being open to learning and not thinking you know everything displays the attitude of a queen, and I celebrate you.

Show Appreciation

No one knows the pain of child-bearing like a mother who has endured it. So then, let it be known that mothers require gentle, loving care. Remember this message, and let it remind you to massage her, the mother who has served you and your children for all these years. Tell her often how much she is valued. Appreciation is the best way to validate and reward a selfless servant. Every mother is so very precious to Me for every mother was chosen to be here, right now, to be celebrated. But, without mothers, not one would be here. Bless you, My righteous, gracious, loving, princess mothers, for all that you do and for all that you have done. You are extraordinary!

May 20

Hello, my outrageous gracious King!

Hello, My child and friend.

Amazing Grace

It is true that My grace and love are radical. This is one of the most misunderstood messages in the Church today. Those who remain under the law, without knowing it, criticize those who get the New Covenant reality and say, "They're teaching grace" as if grace is a bad thing!

The Enemy has built walls around My grace and has tried to convince people they are meant to be poor and suffer for what they have done, when all the while if they would understand that what I have done is enough, they could live in abundance in every way.

> *"For if by the one man's offense death reigned through the one, much more those who receive abundance of grace and of the gift of righteousness will reign in life through the One, Jesus Christ." (Romans 5:17 NKJV)*

Grace Poured Out

I want to pour out My Spirit on everyone so that they will be empowered by My grace and truth.

  I am Grace!

    I am Love!

      I am Truth!

        I am Life!

          I am the full measure!

            I am the resurrection from routine works.

I am the one who crushed the Law, so why then do so many remain under it? Abundant life is not a life of shackles, but a life of outrageous, contagious freedom.

> *"For the law of the Spirit of life in Christ Jesus has made me free from the law of sin and death." (Romans 8:2 NKJV)*

And how could one be truly free without grace? This is how the Enemy keeps Christians bound—it is by convincing them by the controversy around grace that they need to earn it by their works.

> *"For by grace you have been saved through faith, and that not of yourselves; it is the gift of God, not of works, lest anyone should boast." (Ephesians 2:8-9 NKJV)*

But Jesus came to finish the work so that we would enter His rest; then the work becomes the joy set before us.

> *"For he who has entered His rest has himself also ceased from his works as God did from His." (Hebrews 4:10 NKJV)*

> *"Looking unto Jesus, the author and finisher of our faith, who for the joy that was set before Him endured the cross, despising the shame, and has sat down at the right hand of the throne of God." (Hebrews 12:2 NKJV)*

No longer do we suffer in vain. No longer is there a need to sacrifice for sin. It is finished! Now you can do according to your faith in radical grace.

> *"And every priest stands ministering daily and offering repeatedly the same sacrifices, which can never take away sins. But this Man, after he had offered one sacrifice for sins forever, sat down at the right hand of God, from that time waiting till his enemies are made his footstool." (Hebrews 10:11-13 NKJV)*

Grace Deserved

Not everyone feels they deserve grace—that is why they do not receive it. But not receiving what they do not deserve is the reason they need it. I came to give it to them, yet they think they do not deserve it. But that is the point of grace—it is not by works; it is undeserved. I first loved you, but not because of what you have done.

It would be pride to remain under the Law when I, who am Grace, paid for you to be released from it. Physical complications many times show evidence of remaining under the Law. **Release yourself from trying to do what has already been done for you!** Why would a farmer plow a field that has just been plowed if not only to wear out his strength?

Grace is the bedrock to laying a foundation. People who experience radical grace are changed by its freedom and more capable of doing the work, not that they may be approved, but that others may be made free. When you are free—then and only then can you free others. So then, be free as I Myself am free.

> *"Therefore if the Son makes you free, you shall be free indeed." (John 8:36 NKJV)*

> *"Stand fast therefore in the liberty by which Christ has made us free, and do not be entangled again with a yoke of bondage." (Galatians 5:1 NKJV)*

Under the Law

The beam in your own eye is the condemnation of being under the Law, and while under the Law, you cannot help others to freedom. First remove the beam—the condemnation that causes you to remain in the grip of patterns of sin—and then you will see clearly to help others.

> *"Or how can you say to your brother, 'Let me remove the speck from your eye'; and look, a plank is in your own eye? Hypocrite! First remove the plank from your own eye, and then you will see clearly to remove the speck from your brother's eye." (Matthew 7:4-5 NKJV)*

First secure your own oxygen mask or your life vest—then help others to secure theirs.

Old Covenant

Many find their self-worth in helping others get set free when they themselves are drowning under the Law of Sin and Death. What good would it do if the one who comes to save you dies on the way? Be made alive by this truth and then you can lead others to life, lest you be trampled on the ground by the stampeding laws of the old covenant. Are you free? Then remain that way so that many will also become free as you move from the chains of the past into the wings of victory that I exchanged them for. As the eagle, you can soar, but only if you know you were made to fly.

Experience Grace

Remember that My grace is what draws people—not My Law. Once people experience My grace, they will gladly want to serve. If they have not experienced My grace, they will not want to serve others. People need love and acceptance, approval and validation—not laws and rules and religious piety. What motivates participation is the realization of amazing gifts that are undeserved. When you are given a gift, don't you naturally want to return the favor with a cheerful heart? This is the joy set before you. People are only willing to sacrifice themselves for the joy set before them, knowing that it will pay off.

> *"Therefore we also, since we are surrounded by so great a cloud of witnesses, let us lay aside every weight, and the sin which so easily ensnares us, and let us run with endurance the race that is set before us, looking unto Jesus, the author and finisher of our faith, who for the joy that was set before him endured the cross, despising the shame, and has sat down at the right hand of the throne of God." (Hebrews 12:1-3 NKJV)*

The Law is necessary, but only if you know you have been empowered by grace to keep it!

May 23

Justified

This is the day of the new dawn, and the sun has risen to shine upon the faces of the righteous that have been justified by the finished work of the cross.

> *"Knowing that a man is not justified by the works of the law but by faith in Jesus Christ, even we have believed in Christ Jesus that we might be justified by faith in Christ and not by the works of the law; for by the works of the law no flesh shall be justified." (Galatians 2:16 KJV)*

Deceived

Those who remain under the Law certainly would not agree that they do because they would have to be deceived to remain under it. How would one know they are deceived unless it was revealed to them by My Spirit? Pride blocks My Spirit's message, and if pride is the block, humble yourselves, all ye people, and consider this: Is it you who fashioned yourself together in your mother's womb? Where were you when I designed the earth?

> *"Where were you when I laid the foundations of the earth? Tell me, if you have understanding." (Job 38:4 NKJV)*

Do you really have all the answers, or do you strive to have the truth revealed constantly as your daily bread? If you desire today's manna, then let go of what manna you have rotting in your bulging pockets of self-knowledge.

The Cross—a Finished Work or Not

Come out from among the tombs of the Law's weight and be fully free. How can you be fully free if you remain thinking the same as you always have? Is not the renewing of the mind from meditation on My words more than a one-time encounter? Why do you confuse this with the one-time event of the cross? Is the cross a finished work, or is it not? Why then do you misunderstand My words to work out your salvation with fear and trembling?

> *"Therefore, my beloved, as you have always obeyed, not as in my presence only, but now much more in my absence, work out your own salvation with fear and trembling; for it is God who works in you both to will and to do for His good pleasure."* (Philippians 2:12-13 NKJV)

To work out your salvation does not mean to save yourself. How could you save yourself from death had it not been because of My finished work? If I then finished the work, was it not to free you so you could do the work with joy? Of course, you do know the truth now, so be free by it and help others leave their boneyard, and I will blow My breath-of-life just as I did in the first garden, and life will come from what was dead.

> *"And you shall know the truth, and the truth shall make you free."* (John 8:32 NKJV)

Faith Without Works

Faith without works is dead, but you see that faith is first faith in what I did to set you free—this gives you empowerment to work.

> *"But do you want to know, O foolish man, that faith without works is dead?" (James 2:20 NKJV)*

You cannot put works before faith because if you do, you will not have the power to work. If I have empowered you by faith in My finished work, you have motivation to see to it that the event of the cross was not in vain but accomplished freedom in you. If you have not found freedom, then perhaps you should read this again. Will you say that you are not under the Law while you labor under its heaviness—too tired to fully help others to freedom? Or will you be empowered by My Spirit to pick up your cross and follow me by setting aside your own made-up mind and being willing to see My truth from the perspective of heaven?

Sin No More

I tell you the truth: I have the best seat in the house and see everything but your sins, which I have clearly blotted out. Go and be empowered to sin no more by My Holy Spirit.

> *"Afterward Jesus found him in the temple, and said to him, 'See, you have been made well. Sin no more, lest a worse thing come upon you.'" (John 5:14 NKJV)*

If you fail, receive My forgiveness and go strong again lest you depart from Me under the guilt and shame that the Law brings without the full understanding of grace.

Grace Builds My Church

Grace is like a fire—it is stoked by My own mouth and will expand the more you receive it. Grace builds My Church and love sustains it. No other message should be the focus. No other sound should be allowed. No other mindset agrees with My plan to free the captives of their past and set them free to carry out destiny's purpose:

Be free as I am free;

  Be holy as I am holy;

    Be light as I am light;

      Be continually filled so that you can fill others.

The law is fulfilled;

  The debt is paid;

    The requirements are met!

Evidence of Faith

Look for evidence in the faith of others until you gather enough for yourself, but I tell the truth—every act of faith toward the will of your Father in Heaven will be rewarded.

> *"Now faith is the substance of things hoped for, the evidence of things not seen. For by it the elders obtained a good testimony. By faith we understand that the worlds were framed by the word of God, so that the things which are seen were not made of things which are visible." (Hebrews 11:1-3 NKJV)*

So then, do according to your faith in My message of grace. Did I pay for your freedom?

> *"Therefore if the Son makes you free, you shall be free indeed." (John 8:36 NKJV)*

Then how is it that you are not free? Have you accepted fully My message of fulfillment? The Law is satisfied. Now go and obey Me. Freedom is expressed in action, but action cannot by itself cause you to be free. What you do does not prove you are free, but it exposes why you do it.

Paid in Advance

If you work in My field because I have paid you in advance, your work is unencumbered by your debt. If you have the debt weighing you down, then you labor much differently and less efficiently. So then, rest in the fact that the payment has been received and will continue to be. I do not make only one installment and then leave you deserted, but I continue to meet every need because I am the great I AM.

> *"For what does the Scripture say? Abraham believed God and it was accounted to him for righteousness. Now to him who works, the wages are not counted as grace but as debt. But to him who does not work but believes on Him who justifies the ungodly, his faith is accounted for righteousness." (Romans 4:3-5 NKJV)*

May 25

I AM

I am renewing your mind—one word at a time.

I am lifting your weight—one step at a time.

I am filling your soul—one light at a time.

I am clearing your path—one thought at a time.

I am securing your future—one person at a time.

I am building My church—one heart at a time.

I am the First and the Last,

The Beginning and the End,

The Alpha and Omega,

The Prince of Peace,

The Bread of Life, and

The Lion of the Tribe of Judah!

Do you see Me? *He took off His sandals and said,* "Will you wash My feet?"

I responded, "Of course. It would be an honor."

Serve with Joy

You will see My Spirit released this Sunday at the Foot-Washing service. Call the people and invite them to show others to do this as unto Me. When you serve others, you serve Me and I release favor upon all who serve Me with a pure heart—that is a heart with a pure, selfless motive, a heart that has the joy of serving. Many serve to gain, but blessed are those who serve from joy for I, the Lord, love a joyful servant.

Selfish Serving

A self-focused, selfish servant brings shame upon My house. Blessed are those who give of themselves cheerfully. Those who receive from a cheerful giver receive with thanksgiving, knowing the gift has no strings attached. To those who only do according to their selfishness, their reward is lost and given to another. Ask yourself, My people, "Why do I give? What is my motivation?" If it's anything other than obedience, it is done in vain.

Many will come and say, "Lord, Lord, did I not do all of this in Your name?" But those who use My name in vain, who have deceived themselves by impure motives, will be exposed. So then, search your hearts and ask with honest evaluation, "Why am I doing this? Then adjust your heart and mind so that your will will be about your Father's business. Then I will see that your heart is pure and bless you beyond your own comprehension. Do you doubt that I can? Will you believe what I have said? Remember, if you do not believe, you will not receive.

May 27

Washing Feet

To wash feet is a privilege because serving others is a privilege. That is why I demonstrated My heart to serve My people and taught My followers to do the same.

> *"After that, He poured water into a basin and began to wash the disciples' feet, and to wipe them with the towel with which He was girded. Then He came to Simon Peter. And Peter said to Him, 'Lord, are You washing my feet?' Jesus answered and said to him, 'What I am doing you do not understand now, but you will know after this.' Peter said to Him, 'You shall never wash my feet!' Jesus answered him, 'If I do not wash you, you have no part with Me.' Simon Peter said to Him, 'Lord, not my feet only, but also my hands and my head!' Jesus said to him, 'He who is bathed needs only to wash his feet, but is completely clean; and you are clean, but not all of you.'" (John 13:5-10 NKJV)*

Motivated by Pride

Some find it difficult to receive service from others because of pride, and others find it difficult to serve because of pride. Pride says, "I will prove I am a servant of God by serving to show I am great." This is the wrong motivation. Others say, "I cannot receive the service of another because I wish to be the one to serve because all who serve are great." This again is the wrong motivation.

Motivated by Obedience

Our motivation to receive service from others and to serve others, to be correct, is by obedience alone. If I say to serve, as your Lord, and you do it, I am pleased. Serve one another from love and do this as unto Me.

> *"For you, brethren, have been called to liberty; only do not use liberty as an opportunity for the flesh, but through love serve one another." (Galatians 5:13 NKJV)*

June 2012

June 1

Contentment

Don't worry. I have made plans that have your best interests in mind. Why is it so hard for My children to rest in Me through contentment?

> *"Take My yoke upon you and learn from Me, for I am gentle and lowly in heart, and you will find rest for your souls." (Matthew 11:29 NKJV)*

Wanting is different than being in want. You can want something but also be happy with what you have, knowing this is the secret to life. Wanting becomes a bad thing when it keeps you from enjoying the present. Some believe the present is what they're striving for, but contentment sees the *presents* that have already been opened.

Discontentment

Discontentment brings discouragement. I love to see My children happy, but I am most happy when they sit with Me, one on one. Those who long for this will also enjoy intimacy with Me. This is what makes life worth living! Knowing My abundance is released in My presence is a key that has unlocked your future. Load up on My presence so that all of you is full of all of Me!

June 6

Hearing My Voice (Instructions for Equipping Meeting)

I will rock the house. I will bring explosions of love and presents of peace. I want you to read in Matthew and take turns letting others read out loud in sections and then discuss and encourage participation so that each one will learn to get comfortable with reading in public and overcome their fears of speaking out for Me. I want you to teach how to move in hearing My voice and exercising faith through prophecy.

Steps to Hearing

1. Get quiet.

2. Communicate with God.

3. Expect to hear (getting your pen and paper ready demonstrates faith).

4. Write down what the Lord says.

5. Share with others as you are led.

Practicums

Don't show people how big your fish is—teach others how to fish. So many Christians hear so many different things about hearing My voice, but the truth about hearing is this: I am a rewarder of those who diligently seek Me.

> *"But without faith it is impossible to please Him: for he that cometh to God must believe that He is, and that He is a rewarder of them that diligently seek Him." (Hebrews 11:6 KJV)*

I am the one who surrounds surrender. Faith is the substance of believing you will hear My voice. Not believing you will hear is why people don't hear.

> *"Now faith is the substance of things hoped for, the evidence of things not seen." (Hebrews 11:1 NKJV)*

Say something like: "He is here right now," or "Adjust your awareness of His presence."

> *"For where two or three are gathered together in My name, I am there in the midst of them." (Matthew 18:20 NKJV)*

Believe first and your faith will be fully manifest. Ask everyone to cry out to Jesus: "Are You here, Jesus?" or "You are here, aren't you, Lord?"

Will you remember what I am saying to you? I can remind you for I am the Holy Spirit speaking to you. I am your built-in teacher!

> *"A disciple is not above his teacher, but everyone who is perfectly trained will be like his teacher." (Luke 6:40 NKJV)*

June 7

You Are My Student

You know that you are My student, and My student will be a teacher of heaven, showing all the demonstrations of heaven. All who will and all who come will walk in freedom in My house of heaven, released on earth as a forward display of what is to come. Do you understand?

Nathan: Yes, Lord, it is my destiny, and I accept this assignment with honor. Help me be faithful to it.

Walk not after man's agenda. But let Me guide you gently to instruct the great leaders I have prepared to work alongside you, lifting you up from the lowliness of your heart. My peace will be as a great blanket, settling even the wildest of hearts to hear My message of freedom.

Do you want to see My face?

Yes, of course.

Look to your right.

Jesus then shows himself to me and again puts His hand on my head and says, "I bless you. I bless you, I bless you!"

June 9

The Moving of My Spirit

My people who want to see My Spirit move first need to get out of My Spirit's way. My Spirit can only fill what is emptied of self. Those who are full of self cannot be filled. And the filling is not able to be grabbed by eager hands who wish to display themselves. The hands that are put to work to build My house, not a house for themselves, are the hands I will use. These are the hands that will release My Kingdom on earth.

> *"And they were all filled with the Holy Spirit and began to speak with other tongues, as the Spirit gave them utterance."* (Acts 2:4 NKJV)

Check Yourself

Ask whose ambition you are here to fulfill. If you are honest, what would you say? Do you answer the question in haste, or do you consider the deep places of your heart? The Kingdom of Heaven will pour through those who surrender as a way of life, not to be seen by men. Remember, My Spirit is not a store to corner a market and buy stock to divide. It is not for sale, and it is not yours. How then could it be that My people wish to try and be recognized for their own greatness? Do they not know that greatness is only found in Me? I will share My Kingdom with those who desire to promote Me above themselves. Then they may share in My glory. Should man choose who should be elevated in My house? In My Kingdom? Certainly it is only a decision for the Kingdom's ruler alone. Ask Me and listen to My answer.

June 10

Let Go of Sickness

I have come to give life and life more abundantly.

- Do you believe your loving heavenly Father has given you sickness and disease?
- Do you believe you would wish sickness and disease on your own children?

Of course not! So many do not understand My heart of goodness. I did not come to bring death and destruction but to bring life and freedom from pain.

- Do you know how much I love you?
- Do you know I am not angry with you?

Let go of your sickness and all your diseases and I will give you My breath of life.

- Has your malady given you sympathy?
- Has your symptom brought you the attention you want and need?
- Will you trust Me to remove your pain and to heal your soul?

- Will you learn to accept My love and receive the fullness of what I paid to give you on the cross?

I want My people free. Then My free, salty, light-filled Christians will lead others to the same level of commitment.

> *"Therefore if the Son makes you free, you shall be free indeed!" (John 8:36 NKJV)*

Rise Up, Church

If you are a lukewarm leader, you will produce that of the same kind.

> *"So then, because you are lukewarm, and neither cold nor hot, I will vomit you out of My mouth." (Revelation 3:16 NKJV)*

If you are:

On fire,

  All in,

    Committed,

      Eager to serve, and

        Hungry for My Kingdom,

You will produce others who come in behind you with the same passion. It is time to rise up, Church! It is time to be about your Father's business, just as I Myself am. Repent and move in victory so I can advance My Kingdom from your hands and your mouth so all can be fulfilled to bring forth the outpouring of My Spirit as I have promised you.

Let the streets be filled with revival. Let My house be filled with praise. Let the voice cry out from the seven mountains that I am coming back for My beautiful bride! All of you will work with Me to prepare her. The reward will be worth it. I do not ask you to labor in vain, but for the reward of all that is good in heaven and all that I release upon you now:

You are enough!

  You are My prize!

    You are the joy set before Me!

      You are My choice!

        You are My victory!

          You are My love!

        You are My people!

      You are bursting with life!

    You are favored and blessed!

  You are royalty!

You are celebrated in heaven!

Let it be known that your lives will never be the same. Your best days are ahead of you. Your birth marks the divine breath of heaven and My plan for your purpose.

June 11

An Intimate Exhortation

Sometimes My people feel left out when really they are left in. Many times a day I think of you and I eagerly watch to see when you obey My promptings. I smile at your victories and long for the time you give to Me and as you move in faith. I move to open the doors of change.

Walk down the path with playfulness, and let My light shine from you to illuminate the souls of the unsuspecting. Let the darkness find a new home as My goodness shines forth as the sun, bouncing from billows of blessing. Dance on doomsday and send distress looking for a different victim because the access door is closed for business. Conjuring up the Holy Spirit is an illusion to the misguided heart looking for credit. But releasing My Kingdom can only happen through one who has emptied themselves for the filling of My Spirit.

What's considered normal is normally wrong. If super is natural, then it's not normal. Supernatural is normal for those who are super. I want supernatural to be the new normal. Misguided teachers will strain at a gnat, but My Holy Spirit does not need correction. Walk down the back of pride and dive into the humble pool. Drink deep from its clarity until it becomes your measure.

A heart that hears Me does not need to beat;

    I give it pulse to be My retreat.

I set up My camp and carry My lamp

    To fill your table with offering My grant.

Do you wonder why so many will hide?

    They know I am watching, so they hide from their pride.

Pride is like biting into the bitterest grape.

    Everyone looks for the closest escape.

Where can I exit and what can I do

    To show My children humility's truth?

Walk from My entrance and be melody's flair

    So the lost and broken will find faith in Me there.

Do not worry for worry itself

    When you now have royalty's wealth.

Pick up your program and travel with Me far;

    I'll send you through mountains and shoot for the stars.

June 12

Proverbs: (definition: a short pithy saying)

- A gentle rain is like a massage on a dry back. It pours down to quench the thirst of those who find its satisfaction.

- Peace is not underestimated by those under its absence. The piece that's missing will always reveal where the need should be applied.

- Greed is like an endless vacuum. The only way to stop the sucking is to redirect its flow.

- Exhale! If all you do is take breath into yourself but don't breathe on others, you consume yourself with anxious bones. Breath brought life into the world, and again and again, it brings forth life. Every word that comes from My mouth is purposed to raise life from the ashes.

- Glide from the cliff of self-reliance and I will carry you above the rock below to skim the waters of the everlasting, from glory to glory, until all is fulfilled in the fullness of time.

- The clock in My hand is to reveal what is relevant; My presence is not bound by the ticking remembrance.

- The Dove knows where to fly because it hears the voice of its instinct. Greater still will be My shout's whisper upon your willingness to obey Me.

- Where you go, there I am also, and where you speak in My name, I also will be. I am going to have fun releasing through your childlike faith.

- Each opportunity I give will be your springboard, and each time you leap into My water, I will validate your direction.

June 15

Lift the Name of Jesus

Remember that I am your defender. You will not need to waste effort defending your name; just defend mine and I will defend yours. Lift up the name of Jesus, My Son, that every knee will bow and every tongue will confess that Jesus Christ is Lord.

> *"Therefore God also has highly exalted Him and given Him the name which is above every name, that at the name of Jesus every knee should bow, of those in heaven, and of those on earth, and of those under the earth, and that every tongue should confess that Jesus Christ is Lord, to the glory of God the Father." (Philippians 2:9-11 NKJV)*

Speak to the People

The people who come will be personally revived. Those who receive My Sprit will want to leap and shout for joy as I pour out on all flesh. Men and women will weep. Some will mourn the lives of the lost without Christ, and evangelists will rise up with a passion and a fire to reach them. My Spirit's wind will breath upon the unsuspecting, and they will be filled with abundant life and holiness will be their reward.

Holiness is not something you achieve. It is something you receive.

> *"But now having been set free from sin, and having become slaves of God, you have your fruit to holiness, and the end, everlasting life." (Romans 6:22 NKJV)*

People wear themselves out trying to meet requirements, and some finally realize they have already been met. A dog doesn't jump through hoops unless it's trained to, only to return to its own vomit. Do not return to your old stinking thinking, but change your mind, which means to repent so you will know by My Spirit you were made to move, empowered to do great and mighty things, in a forward direction toward the prize that is eternal.

> *"I press toward the goal for the prize of the upward call of God in Christ Jesus." (Philippians 3:14 NKJV)*

Stepping forward to be ignited into My rays of rejoicing is what I have come to draw My people to. Defeat is silent, but victory shouts with joy because life bursts from the healed when before they were helpless. Every changed heart adds tears to the pool of glory and becomes the pool of healing salvation.

When will My bride be ready? When will she allow Me to embrace her again? When will she remove the veil from her eyes so that My face can shine upon her with the reflection of My glory? I tell you the truth, beloved, she will shine brightly so that many will not even look upon her without being redirected from glory to glory.

A changed life is precious, and not one change is ignored. Every change for good is celebrated, and I lavish My loved ones with so much grace and mercy that they want to serve with hungry adoration and great expectation. The power of the resurrection has given hope and life and peace through His great grace and mercy, both now and forever more.

Do you see Me?

Jesus appears in a white robe with a blue sash tied around His waist. His eyes are a bright blue, and He has a lamp in His hand that He lifts up high.

Shine before men, beloved, even brighter than before. Do not worry about your *naysayers*. *[Definition: A person who criticizes, objects to, or opposes something.]* I have given you a big YES! Will I bless you? YES! Will I be with you? YES! Will I pour My Spirit out on all who come to The Rock? YES!

June 16

Tend Your Garden

It is difficult for people to receive My grace, especially since the Enemy is working constantly to cause people to think of their past sin. This is why it's necessary to take every thought captive because you can capture the bad seed before it lands upon the soil of your mind.

> *"For the weapons of our warfare are not carnal but mighty in God for pulling down strongholds, casting down arguments and every high thing that exalts itself against the knowledge of God, bringing every thought into captivity to the obedience of Christ." (2 Corinthians 10:4-5 NKJV)*

Guard your mind and tend to your garden. Be on guard against those who come by it to throw bad seed into its fertile soil. Gossip is like bad seed. It produces destruction. So then, encourage one another's strengths and weakness will be choked out.

June 17

The Covenant of Grace Prayer

Today you will follow My order to bring revival. Lead the people in this prayer:

> *"Fear of man, I command you to go. Get out of me and get out of this place in Jesus' Name. Lord, I receive your gift of righteousness, boldness, and increased wisdom. Lord, fill my heart and fill my soul with the full measure of your Kingdom right now—on earth as it is in heaven. Help me, Lord, to step into this new season of victory. Declare that from this moment on, I will take every thought captive and hold onto only that which is good. I decree that from this moment forward, I will see myself as the righteousness of God, mighty for the pulling down of strongholds and every high thing that exalts itself above the knowledge of God. Thank you for making me in your image. Thank you for reviving my mindsets with the understanding that nothing shall be impossible for me as I walk by faith. The supernatural is natural and naturally super. It is my heritage, as a joint heir to the Kingdom of God. I receive my heritage today. At this very moment, as a new creation, I receive the new covenant, through the blood of Jesus, the covenant of grace. Thank you for the gift of grace, My Lord and King—Jesus Christ! Empower me to extend the same grace and mercy and love to others and to be free as you yourself are free. AMEN."*

June 18

Let Me

Let Me be your fulfillment.

Let Me be your promise.

Let Me search your heart and cause your footsteps to be firm.

Let Me guide you from the dryness of your lack into the season of your favor.

Money Is a Tool

Educate yourself on money and learn how to use it as a tool. I want to teach you how to direct your funds so that your lack of funds no longer directs you. Often, the people who lack are the ones who have made money an idol. Fear of lack, greed, and loss deceive people into removing their faith. And without faith, it is impossible to please Me. Faith always releases with expectancy for goodness. I want to teach you that money matters, and matters of money are often avoided, especially by those who are ruled by it. I want you to be in charge of your money rather than letting your money be in charge of you.

June 20

Sheep and Wolves

> *"Behold, I send you out as sheep in the midst of wolves. Therefore be wise as serpents and harmless as doves." (Matthew 10:16 NKJV)*

During a conversation with another brother, the Lord gave me this vision:

I saw a pasture of sheep with wolves at the corners of the field, nipping in the tall grass. Some wolves were brought in to be sheared—then laid bare and became sheep. Some wolves, lurking in the shadows, were strategizing how and when to strike. Other wolves came and were struck down by the shepherd. After being struck, some turned into lambs while others were destroyed by the rod. Some fled the green pasture to regroup. The wolves wanted to convert the sheep into wolves. As I saw wolves unzipping from their wolf suits and lambs unzipping from their lamb suits, some who were lambs on the outside were wolves on the inside and some wolves on the outside were lambs on the inside. Then the righteous shined forth as the sun and the suits with zippers were destroyed as the light beat through.

> *"Then the righteous will shine forth as the sun in the Kingdom of their Father. He who has ears to hear, let him hear!" (Matthew 13:43 NKJV)*

June 22

More About Grace

One thing to always remember is that My grace is sufficient for thee.

> *"And He said to me, 'My grace is sufficient for you, for My strength is made perfect in weakness.' Therefore most gladly I will rather boast in My infirmities, that the power of Christ may rest upon Me." (2 Corinthians 12:9 NKJV)*

Those who use grace to leverage their disobedience have missed the mark and are blinded by their own sin. My grace empowers and My law sets the standard. A speed limit is in place to give an awareness of an expectation. If it is disregarded, a discipline is applied. An officer can be gracious to a degree, depending on the attitude of the violator. Your Lord is gracious and merciful, yet just as a righteous judge, He is a disciplinarian. He sees the heart and action in deed.

You cannot please Him without faith and faith works. You can tell what a person believes by what a person does. That is why I say you will know them by their fruit.

> *"You will know them by their fruits. Do men gather grapes from thorn bushes or figs from thistles?" (Matthew 7:16 NKJV)*

The fruit is manifested according to works because faith without works is dead.

> *"But do you want to know, oh foolish man, that faith without works is dead?" (James 2:20 NKJV)*

Do My people save themselves? Certainly not. I am the savior, Jesus Christ, lest anyone boast.

> *"For by grace you have been saved through faith, and that not of yourselves; it is the gift of God, not of works, lest anyone should boast." (Ephesians 2:8-9 NKJV)*

But now that you are saved, go to work with joy for what I have done to cause you to be a new creation, empowered by My gift of righteousness.

June 23

Hearing My Voice

Have you ever wondered why some hear God better than others? What is it that blocks the ears from hearing? Do you know why the devil works so hard to block the ears of God's people? Just think about this for a minute. If you're not sure what your God is asking you to do, why would you do anything? If you don't hear God, then certainly you won't know how to obey Him. Imagine if you had a deaf child. You could speak to him all day long, but it wouldn't do any good to give instructions with your voice. You may write your message on paper and put it in front of him, but if he does not read it, how can he obey it?

This is why I have written a book through faithful servants in days of old. It is for the deaf to discover the truth. Those who can see and hear can also learn much from my love letters in the Bible. What I value above the learning of My words is the applying of My words by obedience.

> *"But be doers of the word, and not hearers only, deceiving yourselves." (James 1:22 NKJV)*

Walking out the Bible's life source is like raising up a banner that says, "I am a child of God—a light to this world." Anyone who will come to Me will be filled and the joy comes in releasing what's been given. Those who have ears, let them hear. Those who have eyes, let them see.

I have found your faith, My people, and I am pleased. Use the measure you have been given and it will increase. If you hear Me, then do what I say, for how can you love Me if you do not obey?

> *"If you love Me, keep My commandments." (John 14:15 NKJV)*

Practice Hearing

We, as the people of God, need to learn to hear God. We were meant to hear Him. To hear requires faith. First we must believe that He wants to speak to us. Then we must choose to listen. Expect to hear from Him and then obey what you hear.

> *"So then faith comes by hearing, and hearing by the word of God." (Romans 10:17 NKJV)*

Steps to Hearing

- Get quiet.
- Communicate (talk) with God.
- Expect to hear *(getting your pen and paper ready is faith)*.
- Write down what the Lord says.
- Share with others as you are led.

Questions You Might Ask

1. "Well, pastor, I can't trust the words I hear."

Answer: *You can't, or you won't?*

2. "Well, how do I know the difference between my own thoughts and God's words to me, and how do I know if I'm not being deceived by a stranger's voice?"

Answer: You can learn by practice. The Bible says to test the spirits and to judge the words to evaluate if they are from God.

> *"Beloved, do not believe every spirit, but test the spirits, whether they are of God; because many false prophets have gone out into the world." (I John 4:1 NKJV)*

> *"'And when He brings out His own sheep, He goes before them; and the sheep follow Him, for they know His voice. Yet they will by no means follow a stranger, but will flee from him, for they do not know the voice of strangers.' Jesus used this illustration, but they did not understand the things which He spoke to them." (John 10:4-6 NKJV)*

3. "Yes, but I got it wrong before and people got mad at me, and that was painfully discouraging."

Answer: Well, yes, it can be discouraging, but did you tell that person, "Thus saith the Lord" or did you say, "I'm learning to hear the Lord and I think He's saying this to you"?

Do Not Be Afraid

Do not be afraid that God is going to ask you to do something you don't want to do. If you realize He is for your success in every way, you will want to do what He asks.

> *"Therefore, My beloved, as you have always obeyed, not as in My presence only, but now much more in My absence, work out your own salvation with fear and trembling; for it is God who works in you both to will and to do for His good pleasure." (Philippians 2:12-13 NKJV)*

Do you want your own child to succeed? Of course you do. Will you speak to them to help them? Of course you will. How can you help them if they just keep running away from you? In the same way, God wants to help you, but he needs your cooperation. We are the people of His pasture, and when he says, "Come," it is for a good reason—our life depends on it.

Ear Blockers

Several sins can block our ability to hear the Lord. They are:

- Pride
- Unbelief
- Selfishness
- Unworthiness, and
- Rebellion

If you are having difficulty hearing, ask Him to help you identify the blockage. Then simply confess your agreement with it.

> *"If we confess our sins, He is faithful and just to forgive us our sins and to cleanse us from all unrighteousness." (1 John 1:9 NKJV)*

Now receive the fullness of God who paid with His son, Jesus, all your debts through the shed blood of Jesus.

June 30

Sheep vs. Wolves

I know the name of My sheep. Many who come say they desire to serve Me, but inwardly, they focus on their own desire to satisfy the flesh. My sheep hear My voice because they listen for it, knowing it will preserve them in safety.

> *"My sheep hear My voice, and I know them, and they follow Me." (John 10:27 NKJV)*

Wolves only hear the sound of their own growling appetite for recognition as they rush forward to devour the undiscerning. They gain strength by depleting the life from others. Those who hunger for power are exposed by its snare, but all those who lift up My Son, Jesus, will share in His glory.

> *"Beware of false prophets, who come to you in sheep's clothing, but inwardly they are ravenous wolves." (Matthew 7:15 NKJV)*

> *"Behold, I send you out as sheep in the midst of wolves. Therefore be wise as serpents and harmless as doves." (Matthew 10:16 NKJV)*

Maturity

Beware, beloved, of the motives of man, for many will be deceived by their own lusts. Fill up on My words until you walk in uprightness. In all that you say and do, may you display yourself as mature. Never lose your childlike faith because if you do, you cannot please Me. Liken yourself unto righteousness until those who follow will model the same. Serve the King with diligence, but do not let its practice become His replacement.

Priorities

Watch your calendar and your wallet—let them point to your priority whose focus is being adjusted like the steering wheel of life. Priorities are displayed by actions and actions produce results, displaying what was meant to be revealed.

Dead Branches

Tree branches that are dead will be brittle and break easy, unable to support your weight. As you fall to the ground, snapping and grabbing, you find one that is alive, one that will hold your weight. When you do, cut off the deadness just above the life mark and the tree will live. Do nothing and death will pass down the tree until it is unstable. Cut it down when you find it while you can still choose its landing, lest other trees be affected by its fall. If in the tree there are living things, help them to safety. Even what has been cut down can be useful. For example, it can be used to provide fuel for burning and light in the darkness. Gather around it so that all can benefit from each lesson as you share stories in love and learn to grow in maturity. Every branch that does not bear fruit should be cut down and thrown into the fire. At least then it becomes useful. A crow may land, but it will not rest until it is satisfied. So it is with the wicked as they hunger for the blood of the righteous.

"And even now the ax is laid to the root of the trees. Therefore every tree which does not bear good fruit is cut down and thrown into the fire." (Matthew 3:10 NKJV)

1 Timothy 4 (NKJV)

The Great Apostasy

Now the Spirit expressly says that in latter times some will depart from the faith, giving heed to deceiving spirits and doctrines of demons, speaking lies in hypocrisy, having their own conscience seared with a hot iron, forbidding to marry, *and commanding* to abstain from foods which God created to be received with thanksgiving by those who believe and know the truth. For every creature of God *is* good, and nothing is to be refused if it is received with thanksgiving; for it is sanctified by the word of God and prayer.

A Good Servant of Jesus Christ

If you instruct the brethren in these things, you will be a good minister of Jesus Christ, nourished in the words of faith and of the good doctrine which you have carefully followed. But reject profane and old wives' fables, and exercise yourself toward godliness. For bodily exercise profits a little, but godliness is profitable for all things, having promise of the life that now is and of that which is to come. This *is* a faithful saying and worthy of all acceptance. For to this *end* we both labor and suffer reproach, because we trust in the living God, who is *the* Savior of all men, especially of those who believe. These things command and teach.

Take Heed to Your Ministry

Let no one despise your youth, but be an example to the believers in word, in conduct, in love, in spirit, in faith, in purity. Till I come, give attention to reading, to exhortation, to doctrine. Do not neglect the gift that is in you, which was given to you by prophecy with the laying on of the hands of the eldership. Meditate on these things; give yourself entirely to them, that your progress may be evident to all. Take heed to yourself and to the doctrine. Continue in them, for in doing this you will save both yourself and those who hear you.

July 2012

July 6

Wisdom Whispers from Heaven

My people perish for lack of knowledge, but wisdom whispers from heaven and directs the surrendered soul.

> *"My people are destroyed for lack of knowledge. Because you have rejected knowledge, I also will reject you from being priest for Me; Because you have forgotten the law of your God, I also will forget your children." (Hosea 4:6 NKJV)*

Beckoning from the deep is My wind of mercy; Rising like the sun is the peeking of My light. No shadows live in My house because all is laid bare. Blessed is the heart that turns to Me in fear. Reverent fear can save many lives from destruction, but wayward are those who do not obey. To say you love Me in word alone is to miss its meaning.

> *"My little children, let us not love in word or in tongue, but in deed and in truth." (1 John 3:18 NKJV)*

Blessed are those who resist the snares of man.

July 9

A Touch

This morning, Lord, I felt a finger touch my left temple and a surge of power entered me. I quickly looked up, but no one was there. I asked my wife if she had touched me, and before she even answered, I knew it was not her. I had her put her finger on the same spot, and her touch was not the same as the one I felt. Who then physically touched me? I asked you, Lord, and you said:

You have been marked for greatness.

I'm amazed that this was not only said in the Spirit but it was physically demonstrated. I said, "What's up?"

I came to confirm to you that a change has occurred. What you felt yesterday was My Spirit fully upon you. This was a foretaste of what is to come. After one year of training, you now graduate to a new level of favor and dominion. I validated you to My people and you received this morning My physical touch. Make no mistake that your life will not stay the same. This is a shift from what you knew to what you will now enjoy—My continual revelation that will change the world. Your graduation is celebrated in heaven!

July 11

A Journey

Will You take me on a journey, Lord?

Yes, I will: You are surrounded by a rainbow sea. You look down and your feet are covered by the colorful water, representing My life in spiritual gifting. You walk along carefully, believing that no matter how deep the water gets, you will remain on its surface. When waves come, you concentrate more on Me, fighting the urge to look at them as they splash upon your shins, smacking against your position. You reach for a handle to hold your balance, but there is no handle to save you. I whisper, "Back on Me; keep your eyes on Me." People throw stones from the shore where you once stood, trying to knock you into the water's deep. I whisper, "Back on Me, keep your eyes on Me."

Focus on the Prize

Do not remain afraid of failure, but focus now on the prize that is clearly displayed before you and let My message be the bridge that rests alongside what is divided. Walk with Me with eyes fixed on the prize of your salvation, secured for My purposes.

"Do you not know that those who run in a race all run, but one receives the prize? Run in such a way that you may obtain it." (1 Corinthians 9:24 NKJV)

Colors of Freedom

These are the colors of FREEDOM:

- Blue is for My Holy Spirit.
- Red is for sanctification.
- Orange is for perfect peace.
- Purple is for My royal priesthood.
- Yellow is for the sun's reflection, and
- Pink is for harmony from rest.

A Lifeline

There are reasons for everything in My Kingdom. I will expose those who are motivated by their own lust for power, and you will see clearly what I want you to see. Use the keys you have been given to unlock the doors of destiny, one life at a time. I will walk with you before the attorneys who practice lawlessness. Those men who know My word but misuse its purpose will eat of rotten fruit. My book has not been given as a weapon against the weak, but as a lifeline to all who will listen and obey. Know My heart and let it be that what moves Me will move you.

Lessons

Walking through the woods is like facing giants—you are small in comparison. The reality is that the trees have put down their roots and cannot move with My Spirit. Navigate the forest and be free, for what I plant cannot be uprooted. Do not fear the shadows. You have the sword of My Spirit. Is it not enough to win every battle?

Forged steel is folded many times to create strength. So it is that I have bent you to produce in you My strength.

Water that is running does not become stagnant. Let it flow if you wish to be filled. I do not pour into those who choose dryness.

Decide to live free forevermore and all My promises will be fulfilled in you.

Be what I have made you and give Me back your grateful praise. When is it time? When is it right? How many will remain? Who will be left to receive My best? Those whose hearts are not ready will not be used for My purposes. But those who humble themselves I will exalt.

> *"And whoever exalts himself will be humbled, and he who humbles himself will be exalted." (Matthew 23:12 NKJV)*

Things to Consider

- Consider a glacier—beautiful in appearance but cold to the touch, large and bluish, grand and sharp, but slippery and dangerous. Fun if you are dressed for sliding upon it, deadly if you are not ready for its condition. In the same way, many who are big in the faith look harmless on the outside, big in stature, beautiful in color, but if you are not prepared, you could quickly be hypnotized.

- Barren is the bank of the lazy and weary is the heart of the slothful. The diligent hand will build My Kingdom.

- What is the meaning of life? The meaning of life is valued by what it leaves behind for others to receive. You will have a legacy of royal heritage.

- Security is an illusion to the wayward, but liberated is the heart of the obedient. Rewards are often a focus, but the greatest reward is empowerment.

- A wake gets smaller as it loses momentum. But My will is as a wave and its title has been given: *Rushing the Flood Gates*. (Nathan's second book, *Rushing the Flood Gates of Heaven* was published in 2018.)

- Let it be that all those who have ears to hear will hear. But those who walk in selfishness will be consumed by their own rotten fruit. Brittle branches break easy from their own independence, but those who remain In Me will bear much fruit. Be fruitful and multiply means more than just to have babies. It means to bear fruit that will carry on My purposes of love, peace, joy, and patience.

- A beard that is long will cover a face, but bare are the deeds of a man who is shamed by his own error.

- Wayward is a choice of being, but blessed are those who walk in truth, for they will see the light.

- Problems are temporary, but solutions are full of the promise of eternity. My wilderness is caring for those who have chosen to reject My promises.

- Settle into My compassion and learn My ways of mercy and grace, but do not ignore My correction when I ask you to deliver its mail.

- Persons of interest are those seeking truth—all others waste My bounty. The truth is presented like fruit. Those who hunger will be filled with plenty. There is no need to store up what is endless, but the fearful satisfy the flesh, not knowing if this will be the end.

- Saints who rise up are holding heaven, but those who ignore My call are destroyed by rebellion.

- The songbird sings a new song, and every note is heard by the ear that is tuned toward its pleasant sounds.

Large Ships

A large ship is at the mercy of the water as it rises. Who steers its rudder? The one who has tamed their tongue.

> *"Look also at ships: although they are so large and are driven by fierce winds, they are turned by a very small rudder wherever the pilot desires. Even so the tongue is a little member and boasts great things." (James 3:4-5 NKJV)*

Let me be the captain of your ship, for I know where I'm taking you. I will guide your tongue if you don't take the wheel. The waters are deep beneath My will, and life is found in forfeiting your own ambitions.

If the fish jump into your boat, you should not wonder if I sent provision. Just gather your catch and enjoy what has been provided.

You can't swim upstream when the water mass has been forced upon you unless, like the salmon, you burst above the current. Only by My might can you rise to the top of its gushing. Stronger at its source, the water becomes a willing participant in measuring My standard. Dive into playful anticipation for what will be accomplished in all that is released upon those whose lives reflect My glory.

July 12

Launch Pad

I am well pleased. *The Rock of the Harbor*[2] has left the launching pad. The most fuel is exerted before the rocket leaves the pad. This rocket will surely reach the heavens, and heaven will not stop raining upon its thirsty base.

The Righteous Will Shine

My fury will be released upon the wicked and My storehouse will be open to the righteous. They will shine forth as the sun in the Kingdom of their Father.

> *"Then the righteous will shine forth as the sun in the Kingdom of their Father. He who has ears to hear, let him hear!" (Matthew 13:43 NKJV)*

One Attribute Results in Another

Peace is patient, and

   Patience is pleasant.

      Pleasant is the aroma of favor, and

---

[2] The name of the church started in 2011, now called The Rock Revival Center.

Favor is the result of obedience.

Obedience is the result of faith, and

Faith is the result of hope.

Hope comes from longing, and

Longing comes from desire.

Desire comes from purpose, and

Purpose can be found only in its designer.

The Christian life is a life of fun, fantastic, foundations laid for the children of God.

> *"Of old you laid the foundation of the earth, and the heavens are the work of Your hands." (Psalm 102:25 NKJV)*

Deeds and Titles

Deeds and titles—titles and deeds—remain as gifts unopened for the righteous. Resources are given to those who ask and believe while asking.

> *"Therefore I say to you, whatever things you ask when you pray, believe that you receive them, and you will have them." (Mark 11:24 NKJV)*

Many wealthy fear Me and obey My command to give toward My purpose. I will show you and I will show them, and the provision will be properly placed.

It's NOT Meant to Be a Secret

My book will reach the world, for the world has need and I will fill it. The wicked will not prevail in the destruction directed toward the righteous for your faith is your shield.

> *"For though your people, O Israel, be as the sand of the sea, a remnant of them will return; The destruction decreed shall overflow with righteousness."* (Isaiah 10:22 NKJV)

Believe on these things and receive the blessings of My hand sweeping across the fears of the fleeting. Every page of *It's NOT Meant to Be a Secret*[3] is loaded with sparks from heaven waiting to release heaven's fire—holy, righteous, and pure is the dance of My truth!

> *"He performs great signs, so that He even makes fire come down from heaven on the earth in the sight of men."* (Revelation 20:9 NKJV)

---

[3] *It's NOT Meant to Be a Secret* was published in 2012.

July 13

Children of the Living God (a Song)

Children of the living God,

Follow Me as My Spirit calls, falling fresh upon you now.

Children of the living God,

Come to Me as I lift you up, beyond your wildest dreams.

The newness of your life in Me leaves no room for mourning.

Peace can be a comfort, but to *come forth* is to live by faith,

Knowing that I have seen you.

Thunder

The thunder that you hear is a reaction to what is happening today in the heavens. Many transformations are occurring right now, and much good is happening in My house.

> *"The voice of the LORD is over the waters; The God of glory thunders; The LORD is over many waters."* (Psalm 29:3 NKJV)

Weakness vs. Strength

The weak are made strong, and those strong without My blessing are being made weak.

> *"For we are glad when we are weak and you are strong. And this also we pray, that you may be made complete." (2 Corinthians 13:9 NKJV)*

My blessing is upon those who obey and those who seek My will above their own desires. I honor your obedience, My people, and reward your restraint toward wicked things.

> *"Do you not know that to whom you present yourselves slaves to obey, you are that one's slaves whom you obey, whether of sin leading to death, or of obedience leading to righteousness?" (Romans 6:16 NKJV)*

Give Me your whole heart and I will give you the reality of My whole Kingdom. I restrain only those who are quick toward evil, but those who will to do My will will see My glory fall.

I Am Your Weapon

Put on My armor of gratitude and shield yourself in faith, for I am your weapon of victory.

> *"Above all, taking the shield of faith with which you will be able to quench all the fiery darts of the wicked one." (Ephesians 6:16 NKJV)*

Every word spoken is meant for the destruction of all that is wicked.

> *"He who rejects Me, and does not receive My words, has that which judges him—the word that I have spoken will judge him in the last day." (John 12:48 NKJV)*

I do not worry about the attacks of evil; they are like raindrops on My body. Once I wipe them away, they can no longer drip upon it.

Revelation

Do you want more revelation? The reason is never ending. Bring forth the blade and split open the fruit of the righteous to bear the seed. Then plant more from the nectar and ask for instructions for placement. Getting every new blossom ready for blooming is the art of those who generate holy sowing.

Wayward Thinkers

The voice of My Spirit thunders from the deep to shake up the house of the wayward thinkers. Many come to build up My body, but they build upon their own name, and I will shake apart any house not built upon the Rock! I will shake even those who build what they believe is for My Kingdom but deceive themselves by thinking that originates in their own insecurity. Those who have something to prove will show vanity, but those who seek My will will prosper from heaven.

Greed

Do not be snared by deception from greed, for it has deceived many great leaders.

> *"So are the ways of everyone who is greedy for gain; it takes away the life of its owners." (Proverbs 1:19 NKJV)*

> *"For the love of money is a root of all kinds of evil, for which some have strayed from the faith in their greediness, and pierced themselves through with many sorrows." (1 Timothy 6:10 NKJV)*

Give as directed and you will not be left in ruin.

Nuggets of Truth...

- Run around to prepare, but be sure to do so from a position of rest in all that My promise delivers.

- Consider a glacier lifted high above the water. So it is that all who will be are lifted up by the living waters.

- A cross in the dirt means nothing to the ground around it, but those who understand its meaning are set free.

- What is My Spirit preparing? I am preparing an outburst of victory for all who show Me their chains.

- I have brought and will continue to bring to you a bounty of many wonder-filled moments. Collect them again and give out My message.

- Books are not measured by the weight of their pages, but by the weight of the words upon them!

- Do you have enough muscle to carry what is coming? Of course you do—I will help you.

- Give me your time and I will give you what is priceless—the wisdom of heaven's exchange.

- Some people dance to be seen and some to practice, but dance in the Spirit and you will exercise your soul.

- Proverbs are for insight, and insight will be poured out on the hungry who have asked to see.

A Song

Gripping onto the branch of promise,

    Lifting you from lessons' song.

Praising past the fleeting failure,

    Laying hope on what belongs.

Finding all from searching,

    Deep in My heart's redeeming face,

Leads me to the road of mercy,

    Lined with stones of endless grace.

It's time to pick up what I lay down,

    My voice like thunder, you hear its sound.

But don't wait to see Me when I draw near,

    Just enter in and shed your tears.

Know Me now and you'll know Me then;

    My Spirit passes just like the wind.

Grabbing hold of mercy's plan,

    Just as easy as life began.

"Will you come and light my way?"

    My voice has beckoned, your love displayed.

July 13

Heaven's Touch

Many saints are assembling to intercede for The Rock of the Harbor *(now Rock Revival Center)*. You, in deed, are equipping the saints for the work of the ministry. Every heart needs heaven's touch. Every single soul has need of Light.

> *"And He Himself gave some to be apostles, some prophets, some evangelists, and some pastors and teachers, for the equipping of the saints for the work of ministry, for the edifying of the body of Christ, till we all come to the unity of the faith and of the knowledge of the Son of God, to a perfect man, to the measure of the stature of the fullness of Christ; that we should no longer be children, tossed to and fro and carried about with every wind of doctrine, by the trickery of men, in the cunning craftiness of deceitful plotting, but, speaking the truth in love, may grow up in all things into Him who is the head—Christ—from whom the whole body, joined and knit together by what every joint supplies, according to the effective working by which every part does its share, causes growth of the body for the edifying of itself in love."*
> *(Ephesians 4:11-16 NKJV)*

Do you trust Me?

Yes, Lord.

Allow My Spirit to Come

Then here is what I want you to do. After the speaker speaks, allow My Spirit to come down and fill the people as it was at Pentecost.

> *"When the Day of Pentecost had fully come, they were all with one accord in one place. And suddenly there came a sound from heaven, as of a rushing mighty wind, and it filled the whole house where they were sitting. Then there appeared to them divided tongues, as of fire, and one sat upon each of them. And they were all filled with the Holy Spirit and began to speak with other tongues, as the Spirit gave them utterance." (Acts 2:1-4 NKJV)*

Do not be afraid to introduce this idea from faith. Speak what I give you on the spot—unpremeditated. Walls are not just for walling; they are also for tearing down. Release My portion and remember that I will not be stopped, nor can I be removed, but I will open the flood gates of heaven while you rush them with new wings to keep you firmly on top of My flow. Rushing My flood gate is only possible with wings that keep you on the surface of My pouring. Wrap your future around My abundant hope and let My life become your victory as you rise above the trials of your challenged faith.

Heaven's Portion Cannot Be Contained

Do not let the flow pull you from My breath's wind, for I have released upon you heaven's portion and it cannot be contained, but is meant to be overtaken by its mighty rushing thunder. Let Me be your station, holding on to the substance of My eternal goodness, clutching forth destiny's call, embracing your calling, and collecting My words. Gather up the rain while it's pouring and give it to the thirsty before it becomes stagnant. More will be given according to your faith.

July 14

Concerns

Bring to Me your thoughts, one by one. I will bring you a reward to add to your hope. Your primary concerns are no longer primary when they are no longer a concern! Your focus now is on the future plans of My promises to you. Look to Me continually for answers. I will give you rest. Do not worry about your day. Enjoy it!

Water finds its way around the rock, but to pour from the Rock is My specialty. My pierced side produced water also. My love is a well that never runs dry. Sand is washed away with the plans of man, but My goals are set much higher.

> *"A man's heart plans his way, but the Lord directs his steps."*
> *(Proverbs 16:9 NKJV)*

July 15

I'm getting ready for the Sunday Worship Service, Lord. I'm ready to hear You!

Independence from Dependence

Keep your peace and enter with Me into the throne room of Heaven.

> *"After these things I looked, and behold, a door standing open in heaven. And the first voice which I heard was like a trumpet speaking with me, saying, 'Come up here, and I will show you things which must take place after this.'" (Revelation 4:1 NKJV)*

Lay down all your cares.

> *"Casting all your care upon Him, for He cares for you." (1 Peter 5:7 NKJV)*

Then fill up on My Spirit until nothing is absent from you.

> *"And do not be drunk with wine, in which is dissipation; but be filled with the Spirit." (Ephesians 5:18 NKJV)*

Do you know that I have breath that blows when windows and doors are shut?

> *"Also He said to me, 'Prophesy to the breath, prophesy, son of man, and say to the breath, "Thus says the Lord God: 'Come from the four winds, O breath, and breathe on these slain, that they may live.'"'" (Ezekiel 37:9 NKJV)*

Yes, I believe, Lord.

So it will be that what has begun will continue and every person whom I summon will respond in obedience. Those who do not respond to My call are not meant to come until it is their time. My divine order is given to those who have ears to hear and whose own heart has not deceived them. Today, My Spirit will confirm direction for many, and they will find understanding from My Spirit.

July 16

Building a Church

Total surrender is good, but it cannot be achieved by those who order their own steps. "Lord, what would you like me to do right now?" is a good question to ask when you sit idle, unless I have asked you to rest. The development of *The Rock of the Harbor (now Rock Revival Center)* is a process of using free will. I call on many—some come and some don't. I ask many and some say yes, then follow their own command. I use those who are willing to lay down their own plans daily, moment by moment, thought by thought. Otherwise, I am only their director in part. To be directed is good. If the director knows the plans and they are good plans, then why would one resist it? Unless he lacks understanding.

> *"A man's heart plans his way, but the Lord directs his steps." (Proverbs 16:9 NKJV)*

> *"'Woe to the rebellious children,' says the Lord, 'Who take counsel, but not of Me, and who devise plans, but not of My Spirit, that they may add sin to sin.'" (Isaiah 30:1 NKJV)*

July 18

How to Give Me Your Whole Heart

1. Lay down all worry, fear, anxiety, and stress.

2. Listen for My voice often with sensitivity to My Spirit.

3. Give Me your hopes and dreams and I will bring them to pass with My will to bless your obedience.

4. Give Me your dependence by walking in the Spirit.

5. Search yourself continually to be certain that your motivation is always pure.

You Are...

You are remarkably made, and I am guiding your expectancy.

You are being fulfilled as I use your willingness.

You are releasing My plan, and the mountains shake with confirmations.

You are My craftiness, and I continue to shape you with the end in mind.

You are the righteousness of God through Christ Jesus.

I AM the Holy Spirit

I AM the Holy Spirit who whispers to your destiny—beckoning you from your loneliness, causing you to be fully satisfied in My loving presence.

Wear My love like a blanket of calm assurance, and let your senses become aware and know that I am surrounding you.

Rejoice even in your failures, knowing that their acknowledgment encourages your growth.

Laugh at your faith being perfected from fears that no longer have the right to lie. Faith comes from hearing My words, and faith is expanding within you every time you move with My will. Fear is like a cloud of darkness. Faith is the wind that blows it away, revealing the sun.

Hope, Faith, Love

Shine for Me, son, until your joy is infectious. My face is upon you as you look for love's deposit. Find people to bless with words of life. I will lead your eager deliveries. Hand out HOPE, FAITH, and LOVE with grace, mercy, and peace.

> *"We give thanks to God always for you all, making mention of you in our prayers, remembering without ceasing your work of faith, labor of love, and patience of hope in our Lord Jesus Christ in the sight of our God and Father." (1 Thessalonians 1:2-3 NKJV)*

Torment is released on the rebellious, but peaceful rain is poured out on those who seek the truth.

Climb aboard My perfect plan and let Me develop the substance of your hope. Faith is always increased when you are hoping from love. If love motivates your hope, then faith will release its reward. Motive is the key—it only fits if it's based on blessing's ambition. If *self* is motivating, then the key won't fit to unlock the door. Ask then that My heart's goal would be yours and then you will see My will and open the door to destiny's hope. **Unbelief** will not even turn the key if it's in the lock. **Doubt** only brings despair, resulting in discouragement and depression, bringing hopelessness. I tell you the truth: any package labeled with these words, send back to the sender. Do not open them or hold the content of defeat when I send you into victory's courts. Speak the truth always from love, and ride its crashing wave until you find yourself spilled out on the beautiful beaches of blessing.

July 19

I Am a Developer

I do not throw things together.

   I am a developer.

      I begin each project with the end in mind.

         I have a zero defect policy.

            I build character with trials.

               I build success with failure.

                  I build testimony though triumphant testing.

Be an Overcomer

Every choice is an opportunity to be advanced in My Kingdom. If you fail, you are not condemned but given another chance to overcome.

> *"And he who overcomes, and keeps My works until the end, to him I will give power over the nations."* (Revelation 2:26 NKJV)

When you pass the test, you are given approval to move on in victory to the next challenge. To overcome is a lifestyle from a mindset that is fixed upon My Son, Jesus. And, as the Father God, I see you, My children, as finished, although you remain in the process.

Send the Angels

The finished work of the cross has given you great power to send the angels out, yet so many angels remain still at their posts because many Christians do not know the victory power of the cross.

> *"The Son of Man will send out His angels, and they will gather out of His Kingdom all things that offend, and those who practice lawlessness and will cast them into the furnace of fire. There will be wailing and gnashing of teeth." (Matthew 13: 42-43 NKJV)*

The blood that was shed to fulfill the Law's requirements has accomplished an eternity of atonement, yet the fowler continues to drop his snare before the feet of those not prepared with the gospel of peace.

> *"And how shall they preach unless they are sent? As it is written: 'How beautiful are the feet of those who preach the gospel of peace, who bring glad tidings of good things!'" (Romans 10:15 NKJV)*

Let It Be Known

Be ready to give an account.

> *"And there is no creature hidden from His sight, but all things are naked and open to the eyes of Him to whom we must give account." (Hebrews 4:13 NKJV)*

Write My truth on your heart, beloved.

> *"Let not mercy and truth forsake you; bind them around your neck, write them on the tablet of your heart, and so find favor and high esteem in the sight of God and man." (Proverbs 3:2-4 NKJV)*

Let it be known that My children have inherited My Kingdom and have been given the right to reign in life.

> *"For if by the one man's offense death reigned through the one, much more those who receive abundance of grace and of the gift of righteousness will reign in life through the One, Jesus Christ." (Romans 5:17 NKJV)*

Be continually filled with faith expanding, that all those who doubt will lose their reason to. Proclaim My gospel's message that the good news would shout out, "You are more than enough because I see you for what you will be and through what I have done to set you free." So now, be free as I Myself am free, and resist the devil and he will flee.

> *"Therefore if the Son makes you free, you shall be free indeed." (John 8:36 NKJV)*

> *"Therefore submit to God. Resist the devil and he will flee from you." (James 4:7 NKJV)*

Use My word's truth to send the ungodly running for their lives toward repentance so that when they return, they will see My hands of love through you, my willing participant.

Lavish Love

Lavish one another with love so the world will know you are My disciples and give to Me as I have asked of you, with your whole heart, that nothing will be lacking.

> *"By this all will know that you are My disciples, if you have love for one another."* (John 13:35 NKJV)

Spill over as I spill in and you will overcome sin. Get ready for an increase of the measure of heaven that you have not dreamed possible, and let Me take you where My plans have already gone—paradise on earth as it is in heaven!

July 22

Some Things Worth Mentioning

Peace be with you.

    Walk with Me.

Shower in the glory of My righteousness, and

    You will be cleansed by My wave of mercy's rain.

Diligence is what will bring My favor:

    Diligence toward hearing,

        Diligence toward listening, and

            Diligence toward obeying.

Learning to listen is an art.

    What is most important about listening is gaining understanding.

        Understanding applies wisdom's answer.

Rest in Me.

  Trust in Me.

    Hope in Me.

Doubt not and fail not.

A horse wins a race by setting a pace.

Shattered perception comes from a loss of direction.

A satellite can pick up a signal's sending;

  So does My Spirit gather all the descending.

Rivers of life can fill what's left empty.

Consider a tree:

  It's planted for life with roots down deep,

    Grabbing and pulling,

      Passing through seasons of change,

        Winter and autumn and summer and spring.

I Write Through Your Pen

I write through your pen till no one's in doubt

    And every new lesson, through My love I shout.

Dancing without you, I offer My help,

I invite you to join Me; don't stay without.

Pick it up and open it now,

The gift that sat without even a route.

Walk in My shoes, although you might fall;

I'll stand you back up and help you walk tall.

When you come, listen! My voice like a song;

I'll give back what's been taken, so much that is gone.

I Have Heard

I have heard the choice you have made to overcome, to listen, to obey, and I am pleased with your statements of faith.

Purpose is manifest in action.

Action is taken from faith.

Faith is built by challenge.

Challenge brings strength.

Strength is what lifts the weight of another.

"Finally my brethren, be strong in the Lord and in the power of His might. Put on the whole armor of God that you may be able to stand against the wiles of the devil." (Ephesians 6:10-11 NKJV)

July 24

Represent Me Well

You are building upon My reputation, so be careful to represent Me well by having a loving attitude toward your children. They are like My very own. Discipline them quickly from love so they will not be insecure by not finding solid boundaries.

Your season of change is upon you. Yes, it was My will that you spend time at your new home. My peace has already been established at this private retreat. You will make it beautiful, and I will bring together wonderful events that can be shared with your ministry team and partners. You will be very effective as you learn to work well with others. Collaboration is the key to success. Let Me stay in front as you fix your eyes on Me. Then life will line up just as I have intended.

July 25

Life of a Chicken

I splash upon complacency, and
> Dance upon distress.

I shadow the sheltered
> Who cannot find rest.

I fill only what will empty, and
> Gather what's been laid;

Why, oh why, you wonder
> Are My children dismayed?

Watch the life of a chicken
> Scratching for a treat,

Always searching about
> Tapping with its beak.

Restless nights of fearfulness
> Make it difficult to sleep;

Waiting and wondering,

    When will it retreat?

If the chicken gets chased,

    It is difficult to catch;

If you want its eggs

    It will peck your hand;

If it needs to be moved

    It is better in a cage

So its sharp feet don't poke you

    When it becomes enraged.

A chicken clucks, bok, bok, bok,

    When things don't go its way.

But it is very useful

    If it produces eggs.

Why

Why did you give me this rhyme, Lord?

To say to you, "Don't be a chicken!"

You are not meant to scratch for seed.

Don't run from fear.

Don't let others put you in a cage.

Produce life as you release My Kingdom, and

Guard the seeds and look for fertile soil.

July 27

A Note on Prophesy

Prophesy is a tool for the edification of My body. It lifts My people up. Rather than saying, "Thus saith the Lord," say, "I believe what God is showing me is this…" Pride causes the most harm in the area of prophesy, so be sensitive to speak only from the position of humility, sharing that you are doing your best to understand what God is revealing.

A Paradise Glimpse

Walking through paradise,

    The branches don't break.

Fruit doesn't go bad,

    And you don't eat because you're hungry.

Perfection means that nothing is lacking.

    Every good is within your reach.

Trees need not be cut

    Because they remain within their bounds.

There is no crying

    Or any unpleasant sounds.

No strife, no grief, no pain,

    No furniture to rearrange.

Just pure love, pure joy, and peace

    That goes like this…

All was made to enjoy,

    No longer a need to wish.

What I hope for is in motion

    Like a mystery that's been solved.

I put the life in meaning

    And the meaning has brought faith.

Love is the answer

    To the questions that remain,

Just like a clip of art

    Or a painting that you bring.

Dance upon dilemmas

    And sing when you are down.

Remember My goodness

    And the song of heaven's sound.

It is no longer work

    When you entered My peaceful rest,

And every time I test you,

You can see My heart to bless.

Tramping around My Kingdom

With the freedom that it brings,

Gives us room to wander

During songs My angels sing.

Every time you sit,

Looking around for Me,

My presence is a reminder

Of all you're here to see!

A Trip to Heaven

The Lord invited me to come away with Him to the Olympic Mountains, assuring me that He would personalize our adventure. He led me to Forest Service road #27. I drove to the top and turned off the motor. Jesus asked me to make a list of every promise He had made in the Bible and to me personally. Gratefulness filled my heart as I reviewed the promises of God. He pointed out that gratitude is a key to experiencing divine encounters.

> *"Therefore by Him let us continually offer the sacrifice of praise to God, that is, the fruit of our lips, giving thanks to His name." (Hebrews 13:15 NKJV)*

After this exercise, my vehicle filled with the Glory of the Lord and I found myself transplanted to the top of the Mount of Temptation, located in the Judean Desert. Jesus said, "This is where I was tempted by the Devil." Then I heard the actual exchange, like a replay of a movie clip.

> "Then Jesus was led up by the Spirit into the wilderness to be tempted by the devil. And when He had fasted forty days and forty nights, afterward He was hungry. Now when the tempter came to Him, he said, 'If You are the Son of God, command that these stones become bread.'
>
> "But He answered and said, 'It is written, Man shall not live by bread alone, but by every word that proceeds from the mouth of God.'
>
> "Then the devil took Him up into the holy city, set Him on the pinnacle of the temple, and said to Him, 'If You are the Son of God, throw Yourself down. For it is written: He shall give His angels charge over you, and, In their hands they shall bear you up, lest you dash your foot against a stone.'
>
> "Jesus said to him, 'It is written again, You shall not tempt the Lord your God.'
>
> "Again, the devil took Him up on an exceedingly high mountain, and showed Him all the kingdoms of the world and their glory. And he said to Him, 'All these things I will give You if You will fall down and worship me.'
>
> "Then Jesus said to him, 'Away with you, Satan! For it is written, You shall worship the Lord your God, and Him only you shall serve.'
>
> "Then the devil left Him, and behold, angels came and ministered to Him." (Matthew 4:1-11 NKJV)

We were standing when Jesus said, "Are you ready for this?"

"Yes, Lord." All of a sudden, feathers began to grow out of our arms, rapidly expanding until we were able to mount up on wings like the eagles.

> "But those who wait on the Lord shall renew their strength; They shall mount up with wings like eagles, They shall run and not be weary, They shall walk and not faint." (Isaiah 40:31 NKJV)

He grabbed my hand in His and said, "Let's go!" We flew off the top of the mountain, through a valley, then across to Israel. I saw the temple of the Dome of the Rock and what looked like Syria. There was a war that broke out, and I asked the Lord what I should do. He said, "Release My peace over it." When I did, the war stopped!

We continued our journey up and out of the earth's atmosphere, flowing through a tunnel of stars, until we reached heaven. As we entered the pearly gates, there was a huge welcoming party celebrating our arrival. The Lord released me to explore. I did loop-de-loops over the Crystal Sea, flying around and around with total freedom. It felt like a roller coaster. I dove into the Crystal Sea and found that I could breathe easily underwater. The Lord said, "In My heaven are many mansions; if it were not so, I would have told you."

> *"In My Father's house are many mansions; if it were not so, I would have told you. I go to prepare a place for you." (John 14:2 NKJV)*

He asked if I would like to see my house. Of course I said yes and floated up the steps to the entrance, amazed at what I saw. I could write an entire book on this one encounter. I looked into many rooms, and one thing that really impacted me was a long table, loaded with food—every kind of food that I have ever loved. The Lord explained to me that I could eat anything I wanted to; it was all non-perishable. I ate from the bounty, one item at a time, and as I did, the food replenished itself. The Lord explained there are no shortages in heaven.

I saw, maybe a hundred, angels literally hovering on the Glory, suspended above the train of His robe, and I ran my hand under it to see if the angels were touching it.

> *"In the year that King Uzziah died, I saw the Lord sitting on a throne, high and lifted up, and the train of His robe filled the temple." (Isaiah 6:1 NKJV)*

People were talking without using words, interacting by knowing each other's thoughts.

This was my first Heaven encounter, but I've had many since. Perhaps I'll gather the stories together in book form to encourage people who wonder if there really is a place called heaven. Many books have been written on the subject. The Lord is definitely excited to empower these types of adventures for His people, even more as the time of his coming approaches.

> *"For the Lord Himself will descend from heaven with a shout, with the voice of an archangel, and with the trumpet of God. And the dead in Christ will rise first. Then we who are alive and remain shall be caught up together with them in the clouds to meet the Lord in the air. And thus we shall always be with the Lord. Therefore comfort one another with these words." (1 Thessalonians 4:16-18 NKJV)*

July 28

Build My Church

Remember that I can see the end from the beginning and everything in between. Find rest in the details of your life and know that your family is the family of God. I have you on a mission today, and My mission is to build My church.

> *"Upon this rock I will build My church and the gates of hell shall not prevail against it." (Matthew 16:18b KJV)*

Both meetings today are divinely important. Build My church, beloved, and rescue the wayward. Do not lean on your own understanding but on mine.

> *"Trust in the Lord with all your heart, and lean not on your own understanding; In all your ways acknowledge Him, and He shall direct your paths." (Proverbs 3:5,-6 NKJV)*

Each step you take for Me is rewarded. Each word you speak is recorded in heaven and will bring forth fruit, good or bad. Now is the time to rise, My son. Now is the time to take back what has been stolen.

Preparing a Worship Service

What was off in the service today, Lord?

You were jumping around and having some trouble with focus. The solution is to prepare a message in advance. Then be free in the Spirit to bring it from the Spirit. Many miracles did take place and lives were touched.

I love your willingness most of all, and I am pleased with you and all that you are doing. I am willing that you receive your reward. Did you notice My life was in you in ways of faith? When you looked up at the people and put your confidence in Me, I poured out My Spirit. I gave My message of grace, and I always empower those who receive it.

When you ask Me to come and pour out on all flesh, I hear you and believe in you enough that I will empower you to speak into existence those things that are not as though they are, and surely, they shall come to pass.

> *"By faith we understand that the worlds were framed by the word of God, so that the things which are seen were not made of things which are visible." (Hebrews 11:3 NKJV)*

I am with you. You are as a raging flame willing to be spilled out for My people. Light them up, beloved!

> *"Who makes His angels spirits, His ministers a flame of fire." (Psalm 104:4 NKJV)*

I give you My goodness. I give you My gain. I give you My blessing until heaven fully invades earth. My Spirit will swirl above your efforts in Me. My people are coming forth to receive their breakthrough. If you have not yet seen what you have expected, it is only because there are things that still need to come to pass. Those who lead worship must have the joy of the Lord lest they grieve the Spirit. Plan your theme and Scriptures in advance; then work in testimony and short story examples in order to build faith and bring to life what you are hoping for.

"And they overcame him by the blood of the Lamb and by the word of their testimony, and they did not love their lives to the death." (Revelation 12:11 NKJV)

Let me take your cares and concerns and I will restore your will to thrive. You have been in the battle, but it's time for you to rest. I will give you sample instructions and ask that you prepare for my order by putting systems in place. Work with what you have until I improve it. Then you can move on to the next phase. Use your Bible teaching to empower those who do not put it into practice. Be patient and put into place areas of oversight so that as many duties as possible are delegated. Well done, My faithful servant.

July 29

The Ultimate Treasure

Settle into perfection and be filled by the cave-in of My life upon you. Doing what I empower you to do, from satisfaction, is like liquid energy that will fire up your feet.

> *"From above He has sent fire into my bones, and it overpowered them; He has spread a net for my feet and turned me back." (Lamentations 1:13a NKJV)*

Stepping into the arms of destiny, wrap your heart around My mission and draw near to Me as I draw near to you. Spill out My goodness on all who need My love and they will stand in heaven's release, absorbing My full measure. Bring forth destiny's blessing to relive revival's increase. Measure My standard back to you as the gift of anticipation that will mirror My model. Then shine before Me that you also will become a mirror of reflection's duplication.

Look upon My face and let My smile be the application of your strength, filling up My house with the fullness of joy from dancing in My rain. Hold out your palms and let Me splash upon your shores with waves of mercy as you blow the shofar to release My grace. Faith is as a fountain, pouring upon the rock on which My foundation stands. My water pours from the toes of those who dare to stand upon the Rock of all salvation. You have found the only path to My paradise. Now follow after Me, knowing that you have seen into the deep of My heart's divinity.

Manna was given to all men who were hungry for the measure of My mantle, and you, beloved, will wear it well, made strong from weakness. Let the soldiers march in song, sounding My glory's reign upon the drumbeat of feet made willing. My Spirit will pass as a jet from heaven over the assembly of My people who come together to unite hearts of surrender's fragrance. Deeper and deeper you dive into My words of life. Hope is the tank that fills your lungs with the breath that bellows My song. My bridge has been laid at your feet as preparations have allowed for arrows' removal.

Eat of My tree and pluck of its fruit, and be reminded that its endless portion is deep and wide. Taste and see that I am good and plenty is the reward for those who find it. The branches of heaven need not pruning, for perfection sends this blessed message.

A challenge brings strength, and strength brings victory.

Victory brings hope, and faith swings the sword in victory's hand.

Fear is sent from the mouth of the dragon, but

My shield shall become your strength in Faith!

August 2012

August 4

Listen to Me!

When you come into My presence, I shower you with My life. People say they love Me, yet they do not give Me their time. People say, "The Lord this and the Lord that," but they speak only to hear the sound of their own voices. I desire that My children hear Me because they know Me. If they know Me, they will do according to what they know with consistent anticipation for the reward I bring with Me to favor obedience. Many say, "I love God," yet I can see how they spend their time and money. Time spent reveals the heart's intent. Money spent or not spent reveals also the heart's condition.

Yeah

Yeah! All My people who have gathered here in victory! The Lord your God has inhabited your praises.

> *"But thou art holy, O thou that inhabits the praises of Israel." (Psalm 22:3 KJV)*

I will reveal My plans to you as you seek after Me with diligence.

> *"Keep your heart with all diligence, for out of it spring the issues of life." (Proverbs 4:23 NKJV)*

This world is falling down all around you. As I raise you up, be lifted high, My children, seated with Me in the heavens, releasing from My heaven that is open before you now.

You are the righteousness of your God,

>   Maker of heaven and earth;

>   >   Deliverer of your destiny's design.

Welcome to My favor.

>   Welcome to the victory you have prayed for.

>   >   Welcome to the family of My royal priesthood.

> *"But you are a chosen generation, a royal priesthood, a holy nation, His own special people, that you may proclaim the praises of Him who called you out of darkness into His marvelous light; who once were not a people but are now the people of God, who had not obtained mercy but now have obtained mercy." (1 Peter 2:9-10 NKJV)*

I smile at the slightest victory as I live My life through you. When you surrender everything you are, I surround everything you give. I have built you up with trials.

I am the great I AM—

>   The first and the last,

>   >   The beginning and the end,

>   >   >   The Alpha and the Omega.

> *"'I am the Alpha and the Omega, the beginning and the end,' says the Lord, 'who is and who was and who is to come, the Almighty.'" (Revelation 1:8 NKJV)*

Run the Race

Shine before men, beloved; shine brightly upon this Dark Age and labor with your maker to seek and save the lost and broken. Bring to Me your worries and any fears that hinder, and throw off all sin that so easily entangles, and run the race marked out for each of you, looking unto My Son, into the face of glory, that you will be more than conquerors in this move of My Holy Spirit.

> *"Therefore we also, since we are surrounded by so great a cloud of witnesses, let us lay aside every weight, and the sin which so easily ensnares us, and let us run with endurance the race that is set before us, looking unto Jesus, the author and finisher of our faith, who for the joy that was set before Him endured the cross, despising the shame, and has sat down at the right hand of the throne of God." (Hebrews 12:1-2 NKJV)*

Pick up your cross and follow Me that you not labor in vain.

> *"Then he said to them all, 'If anyone desires to come after Me, let him deny himself, and take up his cross daily, and follow Me.'" (Luke 9:23 NKJV)*

Suffering for a Season

Your suffering is only meant for a season to produce fruit so that many become the beneficiary of your pain. But I have come to harvest the souls and free the captives, by My own hand, of rotten fruit produced by sin. Repent, that your heart will be made pure as I, your God, see you from the inside out, through the finished work on the cross. My grace is sufficient for you.

> *"And he said to me, 'My grace is sufficient for you, for my strength is made perfect in weakness.' Therefore most gladly I will rather boast in my infirmities, that the power of Christ may rest upon me." (2 Corinthians 12:9 NKJV)*

Seek to Be Approved

Do not strive to be great before men who rise and fall, but learn to walk uprightly in all that you do for I am the one who justifies.

> *"He stores up sound wisdom for the upright; He is a shield to those who walk uprightly." (Proverbs 2:7 NKJV)*

Who is he who condemns? Seek to be approved by the one who freed you from the shackles of your past sin and set you down upon the green pastures and pours out living water upon you, now beckoning you into My presence by the still waters of all that lives.

Revival Is Here

Why do you wait upon receiving My revival? It is here among you now. Join the party—there is a celebration in My house! Do you not know that praise unlocks for you the breakthrough that you seek? Give thanks to the Lord your God for what has not yet come to pass, with a grateful heart for what you have received of My goodness, and believe as I reward your diligence in surrendering your whole heart to your Prince of Peace. Do you not yet know of My intense love? I have called you now, so come! Come into My arms of bliss and enter My courts with praise for the Kingdom of My Father is invading this earth.

My Name Is Jesus

My name is Jesus, which means Savior. If only all would know their need. Open the door to your heart and give Me your willingness, and I will burst through you into the deep to cause your footsteps to become firm in the foundation of My truth. Resist the Devil and he will flee from you and heaven will reward your faithfulness. Lay hands on the sick and command them to be restored for the same Spirit that raised Me, your Savior, from the dead is within you now. Why do you seem surprised? Many have seen. I am the resurrection and the life. Follow Me and surely you will not die but will live forever in paradise.

> *"Jesus said to her, 'I am the resurrection and the life. He who believes in Me, though he may die, he shall live.'" (John 11:25 NKJV)*

August 6

I Make All Things New

Shame seeks shelter, but victory walks into the open. My Kingdom is full, and My light brings radiation that penetrates through the wicked plans of destruction. Behold, I make all things new; nothing shall be impossible for those who believe.

> *"Then he who sat on the throne said, 'Behold, I make all things new.' And He said to me, 'Write, for these words are true and faithful.'" (Revelation 21:5 NKJV)*

Occupy the Land

Rise up, My people, and take back the grounds that have been robbed from you. I have sent you to occupy the land. No more can sin reign upon your mortal bodies.

> *"Likewise you also, reckon yourselves to be dead indeed to sin, but alive to God in Christ Jesus our Lord. Therefore do not let sin reign in your mortal body, that you should obey it in its lusts. And do not present your members as instruments of unrighteousness to sin, but present yourselves to God as being alive from the dead, and your members as instruments of righteousness to God." (Romans 6:11-13 NKJV)*

Be transformed into the image of your Farther who art in heaven and allow the full manifestation of your faith to bring forth this move of My Spirit.

> *"And do not be conformed to this world, but be transformed by the renewing of your mind, that you may prove what is that good and acceptable and perfect will of God." (Romans 12:2 NKJV)*

Do you doubt? Do you waver? Does unbelief speak from the darkness? Then walk in the light as I Myself am in the light, and surely you will see that My Kingdom has no end and that every act of faith is rewarded from heaven to earth.

> *"For you were once darkness, but now you are light in the Lord. Walk as children of light." (Ephesians 5:8 NKJV)*

Nothing Is Impossible

Many believe My word, and out of fear, limit its power. I tell you the truth: My love is gushing forth for all to see that nothing is impossible for those who put on the full armor of God.

> *"Put on the whole armor of God that you may be able to stand against the wiles of the devil." (Ephesians 6:11 NKJV)*

Do you not know, My children, that the weapons of your warfare are not carnal but are mighty for the pulling down of strongholds and every high thing that exalts itself above the knowledge of God?

> *"For though we walk in the flesh, we do not war according to the flesh, for the weapons of our warfare are not carnal but mighty in God for pulling down strongholds, casting down arguments and every high thing that exalts itself against the knowledge of God, bringing every thought into captivity to the obedience of Christ." (2 Corinthians 10:3-5 NKJV)*

When will you *see*, *understand*, and *use* the fullness of the gifts of My Spirit that you have been given? When will you *put into practice* all that you have seen and heard that your sword would be sharp and active at removing all that is wicked from those set free by My gift of righteousness?

> *"For the word of God is living and powerful, and sharper than any two-edged sword, piercing even to the division of soul and spirit, and of joints and marrow, and is a discerner of the thoughts and intents of the heart." (Hebrews 4:12 NKJV)*

Watch For…

Watch for religious leaders who use the power of seduction to snare the unsuspecting with the agendas of man.

Watch for the white-washed sepulchers who do not know the evil that lives inside of them from an unwillingness to surrender their own mind's dependence. Do you not know that My ways are higher, beloved? Do you not know I have brought the answers to you? My word is alive, and it continues to be written on the pages of the hearts of the pure and lovely.

You Cannot Save Yourselves

Remember this: I indeed see you, My children, through the finished work on the cross. I do *not* keep a record of your wrongs, and I do *not* retain the remembrance of past sin, washed in the blood at Calvary. Why then do you retain the memory of your own sin as if to say from pride, "I will suffer for them myself, Lord; thanks anyway for the offer." Do you not know that this is the cycle of false religion focused on self? I tell you the truth: You were not made to save yourselves, but I—Jesus—am your savior. Whence forth will you come? When will you put aside the full remembrance of all that has condemned you and every weight that has burdened your life?

> *"Therefore we also, since we are surrounded by so great a cloud of witnesses, let us lay aside every weight, and the sin which so easily ensnares us, and let us run with endurance the race that is set before us, looking unto Jesus, the author and finisher of our faith, who for the joy that was set before Him endured the cross, despising the shame, and has sat down at the right hand of the throne of God." (Hebrews 12:1-3 NKJV)*

Fill Up

Fill up with My truth until you spill over from your investment with Me. Seek after My goodness and grace will follow you down the road of victory with its gentle kindness. Be not of this world, but be about the business of your heavenly father who was and is and is to come.

> *"'I am the Alpha and the Omega, the Beginning and the End,' says the Lord, 'who is and who was and who is to come, the Almighty.'" (Revelation 1:8 NKJV)*

Let Me rest upon you as you learn to rest in My promises, and surely you will receive My mercy's song until all is fulfilled, spoken from My prophets who hear the secrets of heaven's mystery, the great and unsearchable things you did not already know.

A Breaking Dam

When is My Spirit going to stop pouring? I tell you the truth, the rushing water is alive and will not die until all has been accomplished for the second coming of the King, returning for his readied bride to bring home all who have ears and hearts for what is holy. What is coming is a breaking dam that cannot hold back the pouring Spirit of the living God. Release the waves, beloved. Stand upon the Rock and rise up with victory until My love reaches the driest valleys. Let them drink deep of My fountain of youth, flowing from the waters of heaven.

Do Great Exploits

My Spirit flows from every word that is born of My Spirit and will accomplish all that it purposed as My intention. Holiness will reign and righteousness will rule as the wicked rulers are removed by the hands of My angels. Set out on your journey, and know that you cannot fail when it is I who have sent you. I do not send you to fail but to conquer! Will you allow Me to release you to go and do great exploits for My name's sake?

> *"But the people who know their God shall be strong, and carry out great exploits." (Daniel 11:32 NKJV)*

August 11

My Agenda/God's Agenda—Miracles and Healings

I loaded my vehicle with frozen meat and set out to sell. The Lord directed me to an old customer, and sure enough, she was ready to purchase more product. "Where do you have pain?" I asked.

"My left arm has really been hurting for about two weeks."

"I pray for people and God heals them. Do you want to see? I'll put my hand on your arm and the pain is going to stop."

"Okay."

So I put my hand on her left arm and commanded the pain to go in the name of Jesus, and it stopped completely. She had a most astonished look on her face.

"Like, how can that be?"

Again, the Lord guided me to a specific house. They were in a crisis situation because the man of the house was in terrible pain; his blood pressure had escalated to a dangerous level and he was on his way to the hospital. Ignoring the strong sense of fear in the house, I suggested we pray together before he leave, mentioning that God had sent me so he could be healed. With his permission, I put my hand on his legs and commanded all pain to stop, then put my hand on his heart and commanded, in Jesus' name, his blood pressure to return to normal. Immediately, he noticed relief. They wanted to be checked out at the hospital to make sure nothing was actually wrong.

At the next house, I saw another man's back get completely healed. After stocking his freezer with meat, I went back to check on the fellow who had had the high blood pressure. They were back from the hospital and, excitedly, he and his wife said that the prayer had worked! The doctor pronounced that his blood pressure was normal and sent him home.

Proceeding to the neighbor's place, I prayed for a man with a pacemaker who "sweated a lot and often turned red" (a description his wife gave). He was very thankful to receive healing for his heart.

Proceeding home, I saw a man in a parking lot, and the Lord said he had a back problem. So, I pulled over and approached him, saying, "Sir, God showed me that you have a problem with your back and He wants to heal you. Is it okay if I pray for you?" Not having his cane, he was shocked that I knew this. I prophesied over him and his wife, then prayed for his back. When he experienced the healing, he pulled out his wallet, full of cash, and started to hand me some bills. I told him he didn't owe me anything and then said, "God loves you and He wants you to see His goodness!" They were amazed.

> "And the prayer of faith will save the sick, and the Lord will raise him up. And if he has committed sins, he will be forgiven." (James 5:15 NKJV)

August 12

Instructions for My People

You will direct the service tomorrow, involving the people to testify and pray for each other. My goal is to bring each one into the maturity of the faith. Every person who comes has need of prayer, and I will answer the prayers of the saints when they pray selflessly and with expectancy, not entitlement. The attitude of the heart matters to Me.

No person can hide from Me the intents of their heart.

> *"For the word of God is living and powerful, and sharper than any two-edged sword, piercing even to the division of soul and spirit, and of joints and marrow, and is a discerner of the thoughts and intents of the heart." (Hebrews 4:12 NKJV)*

I can see each condition and desire to duplicate My process in each who would be willing. Wild hearts look for evil, but the pure heart fixes its eyes on My plans, and surely the pure in heart will win every battle. Breaking willfulness is a process, but those who surrender all will be filled with the full measure of My Kingdom.

Do you want My peace?

> Let Me develop your patience.

Do you want My wisdom?

> Ask for it each day and I will answer you with its blessing.

Do you want more love?

> Give away what you have been given and it will increase in you.

Everything you give away, more will be given back to you, and every time you choose faith, you are shielded from the attacks of fear. Get in My word and focus on My message. Your theme is hearing and doing. Obedience is better than sacrifice. Doing acts of obedience is the only way to please Me. Open the blocked ears of My people, beloved; open their ears!

> *"Then He opens the ears of men, and seals their instruction."*
> *(Job 33:16 NKJV)*

August 14

Hello, Lord. Your servant is listening. I spoke at Teen Challenge yesterday, and it was amazing!

Teen Challenge

You stepped into the obedience of your faith, and I saw you shine brightly before the women there. It was glorious to watch you move with the Spirit's harmony. You listened. You obeyed. And I will reward you. Keep stepping. Do not worry about pitfalls. Just fix your eyes on the author and finisher of your faith and I, Myself, will guide you along the straight path of Praise.

> *"Looking unto Jesus, the author and finisher of our faith, who for the joy that was set before Him endured the cross, despising the shame, and has sat down at the right hand of the throne of God." (Hebrews 12:2 NKJV)*

Lift Me up with your worship, and I will lift every weight and the sin that so easily entangles.

> *"Therefore, since we have so great a cloud of witnesses surrounding us, let us also lay aside every encumbrance and the sin which so easily entangles us, and let us run with endurance the race that is set before us." (Hebrews 12:1 NASB 1995)*

Run with Me until you receive the prize I have purposed for you.

> *"Do you not know that those who run in a race all run, but one receives the prize? Run in such a way that you may obtain it." (1 Corinthians 9:24 NKJV)*

August 17

A House Upon the Rock

I do not dwell among thieves and liars. I set My house upon the rock that will withstand the storms of life.

> *"Therefore whoever hears these sayings of Mine, and does them, I will liken him to a wise man who built his house on the rock." (Matthew 7:24 NKJV)*

Your house will be built on a stone foundation—a plantation of praise, sheltering the needy with starving spirits. Pour into My empty basins, beloved. Find and fill the fatherless. Share your rewards with them so that every seed will mature to bring forth fruit of its own.

Press on so that what you are writing will change the world. I do not share My secrets with those who do not and will not call to Me. I do not waste My words on ears that do not wish to hear. I am always speaking to My creation, but My creation does not always want to listen. Those who will seek Me will find Me, and the gifts I give are eternal and never-ending. Life is found in living; dead words are not worth repeating nor thinking upon. Dead words cannot produce life at all, only death. This is why I wish for you to let Me be your tongue's trainer as a lion who is hungry for a meal I will satisfy.

When will you live out the full measure I have given you? When will you learn all the lessons I have shown you? Why does it take so long for you to respond to Me? Listen carefully so that you don't miss hearing, for your hearing needs to remain strong for us to labor together. There is so much I have to say to you, and I will not tire of expression. Your doing for Me has been so sweet, and My comfort toward you has given you time.

August 19

Green Pastures

It is not how much you fail that matters most; it is how often you succeed. Thank you for speaking. I will lead you to the green pastures; just come along with Me.

> *"He makes me to lie down in green pastures; He leads me beside the still waters." (Psalm 23:2 NKJV)*

Do you not know what I have said? Walk not after the flesh, but after My Spirit. Let your yea be yea and your nay be nay.

> *"But above all things, My brethren, swear not, neither by heaven, neither by the earth, neither by any other oath: but let your yea be yea; and your nay, nay; lest ye fall into condemnation." (James 5:12 KJV)*

You have done much to seek Me, but yet you still waver. Why don't you just rest on My voice and let Me guide you? Do you not know how important you are to Me? Do you not see My favor on your life? Why doubt Me?

> *"Then Elijah talked to them. 'How long are you going to waver between two opinions?' He asked the people. 'If the Lord is God, follow Him. But if Baal is God, then follow him.'" (1 Kings 18:21 NKJV)*

Bind the spirit of Confusion and Mind-Racing. Exercise, drink water, and run the race. Keep looking at Me and keep pressing in, and I will cause you to receive what you have asked for. Let down your selfish guard and return your eyes to your Father as I, Myself, have done so you can be filled with light. That light can light the path of those I have called to serve with you.

>"*Your word is a lamp to my feet and a light to my path.*"
>*(Psalm 119:105 NKJV)*

August 21

Willpower

Where are you, Lord?

I'm with you here, sitting on this lawn. You are My beloved son in whom I am well pleased.

> I choose to see you win.
>> I choose to set you free.
>>> I give to you what you need to remain.

There are some things I do not enjoy doing, but the things you have asked me to do I do enjoy, so why then do I struggle so? Can I just work for You and be sustained like You and your people have been sustained by Father God in days of old?

You are sustained now, and it is not just substance that allows you to march on; it's willpower:

> Will to do;
>> Will to live;
>>> Will to be all you can be.

Hearing Correctly

Why do I not hear you correctly at times, Lord, but at other times, I hear you brilliantly?

Because you do not always want to hear Me. Many times you hear your own wants and they drown out My voice. This is why you must pick up your cross daily and die to self-interests so that self does not speak louder than My voice.

> *"Then He said to them all, 'If anyone desires to come after Me, let him deny himself, and take up his cross daily, and follow Me.'" (Luke 9:23 NKJV)*

I have asked you to silence the voice of the stranger and the voice of your own will. Do you will to see My fullness? Then, you must first give Me your full efforts.

August 23

Oil of Gladness

Tonight at the cabin, Jesus appeared to me. He held His hands out and said, "This is My oil of gladness." I received it from Him and said, "What do you want me to do with it, Lord?" He said to give it out and pointed to the room. I allowed Him to guide me to those He chose, and I gave the oil of gladness to them. Many received it with laughter and fell down. Then I lay on the floor and laughed with great joy for several minutes.

> *"Then our mouth was filled with laughter, and our tongue with singing. Then they said among the nations, 'The Lord has done great things for them.'" (Psalm 126:2 NKJV)*

Lost in the world of self-focus, many stray, but I have come to free the slaves and turn them into saints. When My glory falls, it is all around, and My life is set to bear the weight of every burden.

August 25

The Mission

What was the will of My Father? To seek and to save the lost, and to go into all the world and make disciples of men.

> "For the Son of Man came to seek and to save the lost." (Luke 19:10 NKJV)

> "Then Jesus came to them and said, 'All authority in heaven and on earth has been given to Me. Therefore go and make disciples of all nations, baptizing them in the name of the Father and of the Son and of the Holy Spirit, and teaching them to obey everything I have commanded you. And surely I am with you always, to the very end of the age.'" (Matthew 28:18-20 NKJV)

What does this mean? To teach others how to enter into the mission of advancing the Kingdom by bringing to them the gospel—the good news! If you tell people bad news, is that the gospel? Of course not! So then, do not place people under the Law's weight, but share My love, grace, and mercy. If you help them receive this first, then once received, they will be transformed into hungry truth-seekers and obedient Christ-followers.

> "Therefore, there is now no condemnation for those who are in Christ Jesus, because through Christ Jesus the law of the

> *Spirit who gives life has set you free from the law of sin and death. For what the law was powerless to do because it was weakened by the flesh, God did by sending his own Son in the likeness of sinful flesh to be a sin offering and so he condemned sin in the flesh in order that the righteous requirement of the law might be fully met in us, who do not live according to the flesh but according to the Spirit." (Romans 8:1-3 NKJV)*

My children, do you not know how much I have forgiven you? Do you not know I gave you everything? Come now and receive your reward of everlasting life, free from the bondage of hopelessness from teaching that does not agree with My character. The mission is to love the Lord your God with all your heart, soul, and strength and to find your neighbor's need and to love him also that you would *be-being*[4] filled to do as you were designed.

> *"Love the Lord your God with all your heart and with all your soul and with all your strength and with all your mind and, love your neighbor as yourself." (Luke 10:27 NKJV)*

Shine back on the One who first shined upon you so that in your reflection, you will see clearly what I have called beautiful. The mission is now! The mission is everywhere you go! The mission is every moment of your day while you remember to represent Me:

In your workplace,

   In your children's school,

      While you are standing in line, and

         While you are driving through town or walking around.

The great commission is a call for those who will, not for just the elect greats. Practice evangelizing by sharing your faith. A willingness to obey is what leads to greatness.

---

[4] "Be" is a continuous action verb in the Greek language.

Guidance

Let My Spirit guide you, beloved. I will give you as much as your hunger allows you to receive. Do you doubt? Train your faith to grow. Do you waver? Give Me your thoughts. Do you wrestle with defeat? Use My sword. Put it back in your hand; then use it and it will sharpen you. Are you judgmental or critical? Then be accepted so that you will be secure.

Discipline Yourself

Are you tired? What holds you back? Is it your diet? Does your exercise routine consist of lifting up your fork? Make your body listen to your mind, guided by your spirit. Tell it what to eat and what it needs to do. Who is in charge of your flesh? Is it My Spirit within you? You must be well to be used in My mission so discipline yourself so that you can disciple.

> *"And have you completely forgotten this word of encouragement that addresses you as a father addresses his son? It says, 'My son, do not make light of the Lord's discipline, and do not lose heart when He rebukes you, because the Lord disciplines the one He loves, and He chastens everyone he accepts as His son.'" (Hebrews 12:4-6 NKJV)*

> *"Then Jesus came to them and said, 'All authority in heaven and on earth has been given to Me. Therefore go and make disciples of all nations, baptizing them in the name of the Father and of the Son and of the Holy Spirit, teaching them to obey everything I have commanded you. And surely I am with you always, to the very end of the age.'" (Matthew 28:18-20 NKJV)*

Love Others as Yourself

The mission is simple: Love Me and love others while you love yourself. Loving yourself by loving others brings fulfillment. If you love others in deeds, you will love yourself and break the cycle of self-focus. Miserable people are inward-focused.

> *"'Teacher, which is the great commandment in the law?' Jesus said to him, "'You shall love the Lord your God with all your heart, with all your soul, and with all your mind." This is the first and great commandment. And the second is like it: "You shall love your neighbor as yourself.""'* (Matthew 22:36-39 NKJV)

Discouragement: A Sidetrack to the Mission

Thoughts of discouragement are meant to discourage. *Dis-couragement is meant to remove courage.* Thoughts of defeat are meant to be defeating. These thoughts bring despair and depression to attack the mission. Remember to think about what you are thinking about with the mission in mind, asking, "Will this thought bring me closer to my mission's goal, or is it a sidetrack to lead me away from it?"

> *"The LORD Himself goes before you and will be with you; He will never leave you nor forsake you. Do not be afraid; do not be discouraged." (Deuteronomy 31:8 NKJV)*

The Great Commission

The great commission is a call for those who will—not for just the elect greats. Practice evangelizing by sharing your faith. Willingness to obey is what leads to greatness.

> *"And Jesus came and spoke to them, saying, 'All authority has been given to Me in heaven and on earth. Go therefore and make disciples of all the nations, baptizing them in the name of the Father and of the Son and of the Holy Spirit, teaching them to observe all things that I have commanded you; and lo, I am with you always, even to the end of the age. Amen.'" (Matthew 28:18-20 NKJV)*

August 26

Arizona

My wife wants me to go to Arizona with her because her mother is dying. What do you want me to do, Lord?

Put a trusted elder in charge of your Well-Spring (church) while you are gone to Arizona and allow for My increase upon you. Do not be afraid, for you will receive your reward. Listen to the voice of My Spirit, beloved. Let Me lift you to the high place. Let Me fill you with the full manifestation of your destiny. I will not fail at accomplishing My goal for you. Just give Me your best and I will do the rest. Talk with your wife and let her see that you are willing to go with her. Plan to be gone for a month and you will have open doors to share the Gospel. I will provide for your needs; one month of your life is what I am asking—four weeks in the desert. Then you will return with the full manifestation of My anointing. Pick up the mantle and mount up on wings as My love for you is brought back to the House of Praise.

Wow, Lord! You have done so much for us all of a sudden! We needed a breakthrough, so I cried out to you, pleading that you would remember your promises from your Word to us. You asked me to submit to my wife and validate her desire to go back to Arizona to be with her mom. I arranged to put an elder in charge for four weeks as you suggested. Then the lie broke off of Danielle that she was second to the ministry. I placed her in position above the ministry and shared with her that I was willing to go to honor her. But she said, "No!" All of a sudden, we get approval for the lease-purchase on our home; I meet John Hagee backstage, and I experience a breakthrough in my marriage and family! We got the house! Thank you, Lord.

Yes, it is exciting! Many times I ask you to do something I don't want you to do, just to see if you will obey. Look at Abraham. I stopped him from sacrificing his son only after the knife was drawn back. I saw his willingness. He passed the test.

> *"So Abraham took the wood of the burnt offering and laid it on Isaac, his son; and he took the fire in his hand, and a knife, and the two of them went together.*
>
> *"But Isaac spoke to Abraham his father and said, 'My father!' And he said, 'Here I am, my son.' Then he said, 'Look, the fire and the wood, but where is the lamb for a burnt offering?'*
>
> *"And Abraham said, 'My son, God will provide for Himself the lamb for a burnt offering.' So the two of them went together.*
>
> *"Then they came to the place of which God had told him. And Abraham built an altar there and placed the wood in order; and he bound Isaac his son and laid him on the altar, upon the wood.*
>
> *"And Abraham stretched out his hand and took the knife to slay his son.*
>
> *But the Angel of the Lord called to him from heaven and said, 'Abraham, Abraham!' So he said, 'Here I am.'*
>
> *"And He said, 'Do not lay your hand on the lad, or do anything to him; for now I know that you fear God, since you have not withheld your son, your only son, from Me.'*
>
> *"Then Abraham lifted his eyes and looked, and there behind him was a ram caught in a thicket by its horns. So Abraham*

went and took the ram, and offered it up for a burnt offering instead of his son." (Genesis 22:6-13 NKJV)

You have also passed the test in honoring your wife by submitting to her need. Then I showed you the reward. Do not discount the words I give to you. Many times you may think they are wrong when they are not. I love to see your responses and delight in your obedience. You are being trained for greatness. Continue on, My son. Continue on!

My Lord God Almighty, maker of heaven and earth! What would you like me to do?

Wisdom of Heaven

Cling to My promises. Ask Me for direction. Give to Me continually your whole heart's treasure. Then I will add to you every blessing that I have promised you. My covenant to Abraham remains. Be fruitful in everything so that others will know you by it and rejoice at what your Father has done to set you increasingly free. Do you wish to understand with the wisdom of heaven?

Yes, Lord!

Then look to Me often and I will give you My eyes to see, just as you have asked Me.

> *"And the Lord said to me, 'Son of man, mark well, see with your eyes and hear with your ears, all that I say to you concerning all the ordinances of the house of the Lord and all its laws.'" (Ezekiel 44:5a NKJV)*

Many would be afraid to pray such things in fear of what they might see that is displeasing. I tell you the truth…seeing in the

Spirit is necessary to operate in the fullness of My gifting upon you, and you will increase in preparation for what is to come.

Our Book

I am funding your book, *It's* NOT *Meant to Be a Secret*. Watch for a surprise blessing, and expect to be increasingly amazed at what I am doing:

I am your provider.

   I am your healer.

      I am your deliverer.

         I am your anointing.

            I am your weight-bearer.

               I will do what I have said!

A Story

Think about this: There was a boy looking for approval. He walked around seeking adventure. He came across a stream and discovered its beauty. As he searched for its source, he could see more and more the effects of beauty in the trees, plants, and flowers. All along the stream was the manifestation of abundant life. When he walked in the light, he was energized by it as if the sun were saying, "I am shining upon your face and My glory will shine from you as you enter in closer to the source of life."

You are that boy! Come this way and let the truth set you free as the pools of everlasting surround your dive of faith. Cherish them while you enter each phase of bliss, knowing that I always save the best for last and I will remain faithful to reward your persistence. Never give up, and always stay focused because the prize is not reserved for Christmas alone. Every act of obedience releases reward and reward is My delight."

Do not tire of doing good, and serve with faith like a child, believing my story's meaning.

> *"And let us not grow weary while doing good, for in due season we shall reap if we do not lose heart." (Galatians 6:9 NKJV)*

You are My child and I am pleased!

August 30

Victory

Welcome to the Victory! Victory is a state of mind focusing on what is working, on what has happened, on what good has come, and will continue to come.

> *"But thanks be to God, who gives us the victory through our Lord Jesus Christ." (1 Corinthians 15:57 NKJV)*

This is the secret to a life of joy. When you put Me first in everything, you will see how I can line up the details of your life to bring forth My good fortune.

> *"You have made known to me the ways of life; you will make me full of joy in Your presence." (Acts 2:28 NKJV)*

Overcoming Leads to Victory

Do you know why I have come? I have come to take your hand and guide you in My ways so that nothing will be missed and all can be fulfilled. Total victory occurs when you believe what I say by putting it into practice. The demonstration of that practice proves the revelation. How can victory be achieved when one does not know how to overcome? I am training you to overcome by allowing circumstances, like hurdles, to train your jump to be strong and precise.

Victory Produced Through Testing and Training

Muscles cannot grow without testing and training. I am testing and training you so that victory springs from defeat.

Develop and grow;

Obey and listen to the voice of your trainer.

I will not fail you if you remain teachable by seeking after My instruction, then applying it to your efforts with an obedient heart. Victorious Christians are the most contagious. Victorious Christians teach others how to overcome obstacles. Victorious Christians know victory's reward because they succeed when the challenge is greatest, knowing My promises always bring forth life and the fruit of perseverance.

> *"My brethren, count it all joy when you fall into various trials, knowing that the testing of your faith produces patience." (James 1:2-3 NKJV)*

> *"We also glory in tribulations, knowing that tribulation produces perseverance; and perseverance character; and character, hope. Now hope does not disappoint, because the love of God has been poured out in our hearts by the Holy Spirit who was given to us." (Romans 5:3-5 NKJV)*

Land of Failure

Is there a culture beyond My victory? Yes. It is in the land of failure. It grows up like a seed in the thoughts of defeat. Defeat knocks always on the door of failure, attempting to steal away the victory.

Stones of Victory

My words are alive and My victory has been won to be shared with those who will respond to My invitation to choose to think on every thought's outcome.

"You can do it!" is a building stone.

"Never give up!"

"Nothing shall be impossible."

"I can do all things through Christ."

Each truth is where you can step to advance, stone by stone, into the victory called forth by your Savior.

Lies also look like stones, but when you put your weight on them, they will surely sink quickly. Therefore, beloved, do not put your trust in circumstance but in the victory of the King of Kings and the Lord of Lords, for He is the victory!

August 31

Can you explain the conflict between Judaism and Christianity, Lord?

Observing the Day of Rest

Yes. There have been many points of division over theology throughout the years:

- When to worship?
- How often?
- For how long?
- In what way?
- On what day?

If the Sabbath is Sunday for you, then let it be your day of rest. Many reserve Saturday or Friday evening, sundown to Saturday. I am more interested in a surrendered heart. That is why I have said that obedience is better than sacrifice.

> *"Has the Lord as great delight in burnt offerings and sacrifices, as in obeying the voice of the Lord? Behold, to obey is better than sacrifice, and to heed than the fat of rams." (1 Samuel 15:22 NKJV)*

Religious Pride

When someone observes their own correctness of deeds above another and has the attitude of, "I'm going to set you straight" instead of "Consider this or that," their words can easily fall into condemnation and Religious Pride. You had a person come into the church who made several assumptions as to what was wrong instead of assessing what was right. You were correct to expose the critical spirit behind this condemnation, masked in holy correction. Holy correction is from love with a mindset of restoration. Just because a person may study the Scriptures enough to quote them does not make them holy. It's the heart's willingness to learn and be teachable that makes one great.

My Spirit will teach you.

  Wisdom listens.

    Knowledge speaks.

Correction and accuracy are important, but not at the expense of unity. Inappropriate correction from pride can lead people to rebellion, defeating the opportunity to win them to the truth. Telling the truth in love is the only way the truth should be told. Religious Pride is the number one divider of the church—more than adultery, gossip, or slander.

September 2012

September 1

Refusing to Eat

I live by every word that comes from the mouth of My heavenly Father.

> *"It is written, 'Man shall not live by bread alone, but by every word that proceeds from the mouth of God.'" (Matthew 4:4 NKJV)*

Not hearing My words is like refusing to eat! Soon you become weak and question what could be wrong. Fasting weakens the flesh, which makes it easier to hear the voice of My Holy Spirit and resist the temptations of the flesh, lust of the eyes, lust of the flesh, and the pride of life, which lead to ruin.

> *"For all that is in the world—the lust of the flesh, the lust of the eyes, and the pride of life—is not of the Father but is of the world." (1 John 2:16 NKJV)*

Time with Me is crucial, beloved. It is the only way to live the life I've given you and to be full to overflowing with My Spirit. You wonder why you are so tired. The move has caused you to become physically tired, but not filling up on the Bread of Life from the I AM is the most obvious factor. Eat and consume My words of Life and you will be increasingly filled until you are satisfied with victory from walking in holiness.

> "And Jesus said to them, 'I am the bread of life. He who comes to Me shall never hunger, and he who believes in Me shall never thirst.'" (John 6:35 NKJV)

Come

"Will you come?" has always been My question. Woe to those who become so self-sufficient that they grow weary of the life of the vine. From blindness, they disconnect, shamefully believing the lies of unworthiness and instead relying on their own withering minds. Even as brilliant as some may be, dying minds become the food of wild dogs.

Be being continually filled until the fountain of life pours freely from you.

> "And they were all filled with the Holy Spirit and began to speak with other tongues, as the Spirit gave them utterance." (Acts 2:4 NKJV)

Bask in My love and fill up with light so that no darkness can hide My truth. Drink in My thoughts as you journal from My reservoirs of resurrection power. Cause what is dead to be made alive and help others fight to win the rewards of faith. Give away faith's gift until the receiver also becomes its giver. Buy back your time with diligence and your investment will be made wisely. Sound is captured in the ear that listens intently; subtle mysteries are missed by the undiscerning.

September 2

Good morning, Lord!

Good morning, son!

Lord, what do you want me to change?

Come to Me in the Quiet

Keep your habit of sitting with Me in the quiet so I can direct you. Do you not know that I can easily help direct your thoughts? Give Me your first thoughts, the fruit of each day, so I can enhance your surroundings with heightened awareness. Remember when I said to you: "I love you just as you are if you do nothing?" That is not because I desire for you to do nothing, but rather that in all you do, you would know I love and accept you. Be mindful of Me during the day. Expect opportunities and experiences. Be open always for divine appointments. Many come to you as angels—messengers sent from Me. Entertain them as you would the one who sends them.

> *"Do not forget to entertain strangers, for by so doing some have unwittingly entertained angels." (Hebrews 13:2 NKJV)*

Overcome the Devil

It is in the name of your Lord Jesus that you are sent, and in the name of Jesus you will overcome the works of the devil, who is lurking around the corners of self-consumption and focus. When you are Christ-centered, it is from a Christ-focus, and selfishness begins to weaken, just as you weaken the flesh by not feeding it. Do you indulge in food as a comfort? Does the flesh cry out to be satisfied? Resist the devil and his gluttony, and he will flee and his lure will be exposed.

> *"Therefore submit to God. Resist the devil and he will flee from you." (James 4:7 NKJV)*

> *"For the drunkard and the glutton will come to poverty, and drowsiness will clothe a man with rags." (Proverbs 23:21 NKJV)*

Do you like to fish? What is it about fishing that you enjoy? Is it the waiting? Or the doubt? Of course not! It's the expectancy—the excitement of hope, the anticipation of something great to come.

When you deny the flesh, you resist the devil.

> *"Then He said to them all, 'If anyone desires to come after Me, let him deny himself, and take up his cross daily, and follow Me.'" (Luke 9:23 NKJV)*

Deny the flesh by fasting and feed the Spirit by filling up on My Word. Then it will be strengthened within you. The lust of the eyes, lust of the flesh, and the pride of life become weak when they are not obeyed. Obeying Me alone will cause you to find safety from derailment. My train is directed by My Spirit. My Spirit has already made up its mind and does not waver. Fix your eyes on Me, beloved, so that your direction will be sure and your path will be straight.

"I say then: Walk in the Spirit, and you shall not fulfill the lust of the flesh. For the flesh lusts against the Spirit, and the Spirit against the flesh; and these are contrary to one another, so that you do not do the things that you wish. But if you are led by the Spirit, you are not under the law." (Galatians 5:16-18 NKJV)

September 4

Assignments from Heaven

Beloved, I am with you. There are many things we will do together—assignments from heaven bring heaven's reward. I am about to release upon you a sum of money. Let Me direct it. I will fund your book project Myself.[5] It will be printed and dispersed and consumed. Many foreigners will be glued to its pages, and My Spirit will pour out to confirm each word of truth.

Favor

Rejoice and be exceedingly glad, for I have favored your obedience, and you will be richly blessed, through My gracious love, to receive much, much more than what you have imagined. Use wisely My resources, and swing open wide the gate of My glory, for you were meant to reign with My Kingdom, strong and precisely, into the flow of My endless love, pouring from the heart of your willing Father who does not keep a record of wrong, but empowers the surrendered to do great and mighty works with willing hands, cleansed by the righteousness of God. Let Me live through you fully and be free. Set My people free and I will tell the story through your mouth and direct your tongue

---

5   *It's* NOT *Meant to Be a Secret* was published in 2012.

to speak with the authority of Heaven. Bursting forth is a new measure of abundant life. Will you come to Me and let Me place upon you another mission?

Yes, Lord, El Shaddai.

A Mission

It is My desire that you go Saturday and see Pastor Mark in the evening to speak to him the words I give you for the Church of All Nations. He is one I have chosen to help you as you help him to return to childlike faith and freedom to move with My Spirit's song. Renew his joy, beloved. Renew his focus. Cause him to enter My rest and embrace his wisdom for your vision. He will embrace you, for he sees as you do and he will know that I have sent you. You will be welcomed and taken under many wings as you walk in faith. Your feet will look for a place to land, but you do not need to worry. I will touch you down when I choose. Do as I say and the wind will confirm your direction.

I Am

I, the Lord God Almighty, the ruler of every nation, will exalt you and you will not be denied access.

I am your vindication.

   I am your rite of passage.

      I am your peace covering.

         I am the joy set before you and upon you.

           I am your quiet confidence.

              I am the word you speak.

                 I am your chain breaker.

I am your founder.

I am your provision.

I am the ruler of your soul.

Be Who I Have Said You Are

Be now, as I have said, mighty in the land, and enter it with the joy of ownership until all is fulfilled that was spoken to the prophets. Nations will tremble at the sound of My voice in you. Crush the head of the seducing spirit of Satan and watch Me burst from you like rushing waters carving out new charts of fruitfulness.

> *"And the God of peace will crush Satan under your feet shortly. The grace of our Lord Jesus Christ be with you. Amen." (Romans 16:20 NKJV)*

These things I say to you are meant to prepare you and for no other purpose. You know who you are not. Be who I have said you are:

Bold,

   Outrageously contagious,

     Prosperous beyond compare,

        A rescuer of those I have chosen,

           One who plucks to freedom those I have called,

        Activator of deaf ears,

     Chain breaker of the addicted,

   Fortress bearer for the King of Kings, and

Royal and righteous with the fullness of life I have bestowed upon you.

I Am Your Friend

Do not waver, but move steadfastly into your season to claim the land that is your inheritance and see My abundance upon your prosperous soul. Get My staff and bring it to Me as I guide you to correct the wayward leaders who pride themselves in keeping the law and we together will free them, one by one, from religious spirits of the Antichrist. See into the keyhole of this door and unlock it with the revelation I have given you. Turn the key and hear the sound of the clicking lock. Watch it open before you riches and glory and power to fulfill your destiny in Me, El Shaddai.

I do not desire defeat from a mindset of reason. I desire breakthrough and blessing and honor. Be lifted up as you focus onward. You do not hear the voice of your own desire but the voice of My Spirit to reveal My direction. You have sought Me with diligence, and I am your reward. Written on the pages of your heart are the ancient stories that have brought much freedom. Do not fear persecution. Just pray and remember that not one weapon set against you can prosper until it is time for Me to bring you home from this fallen world of selfishness.

> *"No weapon formed against you shall prosper, and every tongue which rises against you in judgment you shall condemn. This is the heritage of the servants of the Lord, and their righteousness is from Me, says the Lord." (Isaiah 54:17 NKJV)*

I am your friend and you are dear to My heart, My child whom I have named Nathan.

> *"No longer do I call you servants, for a servant does not know what his master is doing; but I have called you friends, for all things that I heard from My Father I have made known to you." (John 15:15 NKJV)*

You are My precious child, and we are intimately acquainted, and in that intimacy I have caused you to become a strong tower of boldness. You will be My weapon against the Enemy's plan and the gates of hell will not prevail against you.

> *"And I say also unto thee, that thou art Peter, and upon this rock I will build My church; and the gates of hell shall not prevail against it." (Matthew 16:18 KJV)*

You will lead a mighty move of My Spirit in rushing the flood gates of heaven.[6] Let no man take My place, for I am the lamp at your feet, leading you through the darkness of a fallen age. You will shine forth as the sun as we walk together, both here and now and then and forever.

In the quiet, still places of your heart, My voice speaks and you gather its whisper, like fresh manna from heaven. My Spirit provides your soul's food, filling you up not to consume but to prepare to pour out what I have freely poured in. New wine is grace, and gracious I am to free each slave with a heart chained by sin. Now that you are free, child, help others to know the shelter of My freedom.

---

6 *Rushing the Flood Gates of Heaven* was published in 2018.

September 13

Run the Race

People of victory, why would anyone take weight with them to a race, then bring it toward the finish line as if it would help to be loaded up and weighted down to win? I tell you the truth again, throw off the sin that so easily entangles you and run as though you believe you were made to win, lest you fall on your face under the heaviness and trip those running behind you.

> *"Therefore we also, since we are surrounded by so great a cloud of witnesses, let us lay aside every weight, and the sin which so easily ensnares us, and let us run with endurance the race that is set before us, looking unto Jesus, the author and finisher of our faith, who for the joy that was set before Him endured the cross, despising the shame, and has sat down at the right hand of the throne of God. For consider Him who endured such hostility from sinners against Himself, lest you become weary and discouraged in your souls." (Hebrews 12:1-3 NKJV)*

Whose Plans?

Is the race of each runner not observed by many? Of course it is. So stay on course by determining what hinders and snares, and throw it down and away from you to face the challenge. Or do you not plan to win when you plan? Or do you not plan at all? My plans are made and they are good plans. Why then do you, My people, make your own plans as if I have none? Ask Me to reveal My plans as you would look to the experience of an event planner who has planned for a certain similar event and we can work together. As you put Me first, I will direct you with My blessing as I search your heart's posture and approve its intent.

> *"In all your ways acknowledge Him, and He shall direct your paths." (Proverbs 3:6 NKJV)*

Whose Will?

Whose will are you after? I cannot be fooled. Search your hearts, My people, and ask Me to reveal the truth about their motives so you can find plans that are approved, lest you toil in vain.

> *"Search me, O God, and know my heart; try me, and know my anxieties; and see if there is any wicked way in me, and lead me in the way everlasting." (Psalm 139:23-24 NKJV)*

Many wish My blessing upon their plans when they are made apart from Me. I tell you the truth: What comes from fire is pure but what cannot pass through is selfishness and conceit. Will you, My children, claim the land that is waiting for you and invite others to add to its promise? Everyone who seeks finds, and for they who knock, the door will be opened.

> *"For everyone who asks receives, and he who seeks finds, and to him who knocks it will be opened." (Matthew 7:8 NKJV)*

What Can I Do?

Do you ask, "What will be done for me?" or "What can I do?" I judge the thoughts and the attitudes of the heart.

> *"For the word of God is living and powerful, and sharper than any two-edged sword, piercing even to the division of soul and spirit, and of joints and marrow, and is a discerner of the thoughts and intents of the heart." (Hebrews 4:12 NKJV)*

It is I who justifies. Who are they who condemn? It is written, "Man does not live on bread alone but on every word that comes from the mouth of the Father."

> *"But He answered and said, 'It is written, "Man shall not live by bread alone, but by every word that proceeds from the mouth of God."'" (Matthew 4:4 NKJV)*

Feast upon My words so that your mind will be renewed; then you can make decisions—not from the flesh that screams to be satisfied, but from My Spirit within you—the renewed mind of Christ.

> *"Let this mind be in you which was also in Christ Jesus." (Philippians 2:3 NKJV)*

Will you do what I say so your love will be proved, or will you say you love Me in words that are empty? How can hollow words impact a stone? Let your Rock drive forward through the wall of deceit as the stones cry out through the darkness that cannot hide My light, and come to the house where My Spirit is set to pour. Let My favor give you the flavor of one who is salty to bring forth a great thirst and I will shine forth as the sun, ever brighter upon the face of the redeemed. Then you will see the full manifestation of My glory, both now and in the heavens, as you are lost in the flow, rushing the flood gates of heaven, with the full force of My Kingdom!

Lift Up the Son

I, the King of Kings and Lord of Lords, shall reign forever and ever. Receive Me and lift Me from the crowd of your cluttered hearts and shine from My house of light. Lift up the Son and the sun will shine brighter and brighter as He arises to cover the mountains and shadow the wicked who hide their faces and refuse My good measure. Pull the willing to safety, but leave behind those who refuse to walk. Continue on and be strong in your Lord, for He has brought you to the third day.

It is the hour of My awakening!

  It is the moment of My message

    To be transformed into the image of your God;

      To reflect what is holy.

Let your face be My reflection as the windows to your souls are cleansed by tears of great joy from the expectation of what I Myself have promised. Reap with Me the mighty harvest that will be a feast made from the table of the wicked. Remember no more what has been set against you, but cling to Me, My beloved children, with everything you are. Let go of everything you have by putting Me first, and surely you will gain the Kingdom of your God, to share in its great riches. You will lack for nothing good until that day that you enter My gates with the fullness of thanksgiving.

You Are My Inheritance

Royalty is from faith, and faith releases so I can do My part to open the windows of heaven, bringing forth the four winds. You are My inheritance and I am yours.

> *"Then he said, 'If now I have found grace in your sight, O Lord, let my Lord, I pray, go among us, even though we are a stiff-necked people; and pardon our iniquity and our sin, and take us as your inheritance.'" (Exodus 34:9 NKJV)*

Be one with each other as your Father, My Son, and the blessed Holy Spirit are also one. *Unite*, My people!

September 14

Lord, you are a defender of the weak and a shelter for the meek. Thank you, God, for your love.

A Garden

It's time that I take you deeper:

  Deeper into love;

    Deeper into discovery;

      Deeper into understanding.

Wild oats and barley are wild because man did not plant them—I did! The only things planted by man are those things transplanted. I say this because you do not need to plant what has already been sown. Just tend to it as you would your passions. My passion is My creation. I made it and I love to maintain it! Everyone is My project, and every project will be completed.

Do you know what kind of garden you have? Are you tending to its fruit? Biting on an apple is how you taste it. You don't know what it is like until you do. Oh, taste and see that the Lord is good!

> *"Oh, taste and see that the Lord is good; blessed is the man who trusts in Him!" (Psalm 34:8 NKJV)*

September 15

Imprisoned

I will not be mocked. Whatever a man sows, that also he shall reap.

> *"Do not be deceived, God is not mocked; for whatever a man sows, that he will also reap." (Galatians 6:7 NKJV)*

My children are imprisoned by their sin, not because the cell is locked, but because they do not know that it is open. Four walls:

1. Guilt,

2. Shame,

3. Condemnation, and

4. Unworthiness.

Push them over and don't take the bait. Nothing is holding the bars together but illusion. You are free, and whom the Son sets free is free indeed.

> *"Therefore if the Son makes you free, you shall be free indeed." (John 8:36 NKJV)*

Grace, mercy, love, and worthiness bring down the bars.

September 18

Stay on My Path

Yesterday was a significant day of breakthrough. I sent someone to minister to you, and he was blessed as a result of his obedience. Your wife will hear Me, and she will know Me and My thoughts will become her thoughts as I take her deeper into My Kingdom.

Learn the meaning of these words:

> RHEMA – God's Word spoken to you.
>
> PNEUMA – Air in motion (breath) as something necessary to life; Spirit.
>
> ROSHA – A Persian name for girls meaning light or brightness.
>
> MANTA – A blanket that is used as a cloak or shawl.

There's a dirt road near Jerusalem that is very windy. It curves back and forth and goes up and down. It's hard to tell which direction it's going. So many have tried to take shortcuts, hoping to get to the temple quicker, but they miss some very significant attractions along the way. It is My will that your journey be maximized so you will have the greatest impact. Stay on My path and enjoy each turn of development, for this is the path to My Holy city and you will arrive in due time, for I can see much that you cannot, and I, your God, enjoy releasing upon you favor. Walk with expectancy; walk with certainty, and be in remembrance of Me as you do as I have instructed you.

September 19

Teach Victory

Beloved, do not be concerned about making *it* happen. I am the Lord, and I will bring about My bounty. Just seek Me and do what I ask of you, and you will be blessed. I will not stop advancing My Kingdom until all is fulfilled. Be holy, My child, and walk in freedom and teach victory wherever you go. Follow My precepts and march on with the sound of My trumpet!

> *"But as He who called you is holy, you also be holy in all your conduct." (1 Peter 1:15 NKJV)*

> *"For whatever is born of God overcomes the world. And this is the victory that has overcome the world—our faith." (1 John 5:4 NKJV)*

September 20 –
Word to a Christian Leader

My Beloved

My Beloved, My scholar and friend: Life grows busier and busier as you press toward the goal. Thank you for maturing the saints. Thank you for serving Me with diligence. Do not ignore My beckoning. I am calling you to Myself in a deeper way than you have imagined. Give Me more of your time. Fill up on My presence and you will enter again into My rest. Then you will labor from grace to do the increasing work of My Kingdom. My Spirit will guide you in a new way toward a balanced effort of co-laboring.

You Will Prophesy

It is the desire of your God that you see, even as your wife can see, and so it is that you will prophesy and My voice will rise up within you to bring forth the flood of heaven that your soul cries out for. Be who I have made you. Rise up, beloved; rise up from your hunger and let My Spirit pour from your obedience, that all will see there is a God in heaven who is invading earth to bring forth a move of My Spirit that has not yet been seen. It is

My passion within you that has driven your success. I have given to you according to your heart's condition. I am tearing down the walls of all division and rising up a standard that cannot be ignored! Be who I have made you, beloved. Let Me fill you with My increase, for it is not of this world, but from My Spirit says the Lord your God.

A Voice to the Nations

A voice to the nations is what I have said, and a voice to the nations is what you shall be. Rest, beloved; rest in Me; then you will enter My effortlessness and work will become the joy set before you as it was the joy set before Me.

> *"Therefore we also, since we are surrounded by so great a cloud of witnesses, let us lay aside every weight, and the sin which so easily ensnares us, and let us run with endurance the race that is set before us, looking unto Jesus, the author and finisher of our faith, who for the joy that was set before him endured the cross, despising the shame, and has sat down at the right hand of the throne of God." (Hebrews 12:1-3 NKJV)*

I accept you and love you; you have My full approval. Ask of Me and it shall be done on earth as it is in heaven.

My spiritual gifts are available to you;

   My armor is your safety;

     My heart beats for souls;

        My life is for releasing.

Will you let Me have My way?

   Will you go where I send you?

     Will you allow My full measure?

Come to Me, My child, and do not be burdened by the task of coming, but be-being filled as I reach through you to touch the lives who hunger.

Fill Up Again

I see you sitting and asking Me to help you make many important choices. I tell you the truth—My presence is your reward as every good and perfect gift is released from My love.

> *"Every good gift and every perfect gift is from above, and comes down from the Father of lights, with whom there is no variation or shadow of turning." (James 1:17 NKJV)*

Fill up again, and then continue to pour until all is fulfilled by the voice of My prophet's shout with joy, and recall what I have promised you and all will come to pass. That is your destiny as we reign together in one accord to release the captives of self-focus.

Bring Two Cultures Together

Finish the book and release its measure for My will is to use its resource to bring back what was lost and tear down what was meant to dilute it. Bridge the gap and bring two cultures together for the sake of the cross, and I will be increasingly upon you in Spirit and in Truth. Be free in My grace for it is sufficient for you; then walk from the freedom of the new rest I have given you now.

It's not about what you do as much as what has been done.

  It's not about what you have become;

    It's about what I have made you.

      It's not about who you are;

        It's about who I am within you.

Come

Come to My table and sit with Me and I will share with you the details of My heart and what moves it, and you, too, will be moved by such things. Gather what's been scattered and let Me increase your faith and expand My Kingdom within you, even to the ends of the earth. Pencil Me into your schedule again, and give Me the first fruits of your day as you used to do.

September 22

El Shaddai

I am with you in Spirit and in truth. Let not the ways of man become your custom, but learn of Me and I will break their mold. My will cannot be found in self-reliance, only in total dependence on Me. Bring to Me the lost sheep that have been scattered, and I will make them treasures.

Do you know what time it is in the Spirit? Do you know what hour it is? I will fulfill My purpose to bring unity to this land, and I will tear down all false structures until only what I, Myself, have built will stand. I am shaping. I am directing. I am not feeble, nor have I lost My way. I am El Shaddai! I am victory!

September 24

Things to Remember

It is I, the Lord your God, who knows the depths of your heart. Remember Me as I lift you to new heights of success. Remember what you have been through so you can relate to those who endure. Every step will be filled with purpose. Like stepping in soft sand, you will leave a footprint behind that can be followed by those who will come before the passing tide washes away its imprint. Many wish to know the way but cannot find it because they will not get real with themselves about what drives them.

Selfishness, taken from hearts of surrender, will be washed away.

Hopelessness will be removed by waves of faith, hope, and love.

Unworthiness will be cast into the sea, and

Pride will sink down like a millstone, sinking the ships of the wicked.

Righteousness will be given like a life preserver to those who humbly believe. My Spirit looks for the postured heart that will trust and obey.

> *"Who among you fears the Lord? Who obeys the voice of His Servant? Who walks in darkness and has no light? Let*

him trust in the name of the Lord and rely upon his God."
(Isaiah 50:10 NKJV)

A New Song

Lord, will You lead me? Lord, I know You see me.

Lord, do You need me the way I know I need You?

So many choices; so many voices, speaking in so many ways,

But You are who You say you are, so I will seek You first that Your will be done.

Oh, Master of my heart; Come lead, Master of my heart.

I come to You, oh lover of my soul; Come and live in me.

I give you place to be My Lord of all.

September 25

My Goodness Alone

Remember Me when you're walking. Remember that I am with you and that I will not leave you. My hope is within you. My cup I have filled before you, and it will pour out as you hold it in your hands. Rescue the wayward thinkers of self-reliance and grip only what is good, for wisdom's season is balanced. People need change but fear it. Stagnant waters become dangerous; no life can populate them unless they pour out what I pour in. Releasing first is the key to making room for more. Then you can see the life of abundance. My hope is you will receive what I have desired to give. My giving is from My goodness alone.

Transition

You are experiencing a transitional period. I want to bring you into a new depth of awareness in My Spirit.

Okay, Lord.

A Broad Perspective

When you fast, you weaken the flesh so that it does not interfere with My Spirit and the Holy Spirit within you becomes better able to send messages with clarity. Everything I do is on purpose, deliberate, and on time. You may wonder why I do certain things a certain way. The Truth sees the whole picture. I make decisions and actions based on a very broad perspective because I can see the beginning from the end.

> *"'I am the Alpha and the Omega, the Beginning and the End,' says the Lord, 'who is and who was and who is to come, the Almighty!'" (Revelation 1:8 NKJV)*

My Words Are Simple

You are free to choose, but I can see the connection between each choice's outcomes. Don't overthink My words; they are simple and simply put for you to understand with certainty. Give room for error and expect to grow, for My will is perfect and My song is sweet. Flow in My Spirit like a melody, dancing on the frequency of My voice. Hear Me and listen well. Then prove your mission is to obey.

Serving Others Brings Joy

Too many people live for themselves, but as they learn to serve others, they get filled with My joy.

Do you know what makes humor humorous? It's the expectation that it will be. People go to a comic, expecting to laugh. So it is with Me, son. I made you to enjoy you, and I do. I laugh over you all the time.

> *"The Lord your God in your midst, The Mighty One, will save; He will rejoice over you with gladness, He will quiet you with His love, He will rejoice over you with singing." (Zephaniah 3:17 NKJV)*

Be who I have made you and I will release upon you the goodness of My love.

A canary has a beautiful song and a dove hums a tune, but your song is heard in heaven because of who I made you.

Be filled with faith, beloved. Drink deep of what's alive, and I will steady your course and adjust your schedule to fit My plan.

September 27

What would you like me to do, Lord?

Prepare for the Harvest

Prepare the soil for the pouring. I am the till; you are the salt. I am the rain. Shine your light and we will harvest together.

> *"Then He said to His disciples, 'The harvest truly is plentiful, but the laborers are few.'" (Matthew 9:37 NKJV)*

Words to Ponder

Peace is gently flowing water

    Over rocks in need of shaping.

Pristine pools emerge from

    Filling up on what is pure.

Reflections are seen upon the twinkling scape;

    Nothing hides its face and shame is washed away.

Presence is the reward

For all who are captured by it.

Place your hands in My water and be filled with My breeze
> Until your breath is freshened with creation's mint.

From the press to the pedestal, I will display good measure,
> Springing up within you is the everlasting.

My Spirit cannot lose its way,
> Washing your mind and cleansing your soul to embrace a brand new day.

Wrap My joy around despair with your loving arms, and
> Speak to the seas and calm the raging storms.

Peaks and valleys far between but many left untold;
> I will bring you to the source of all that is upright and bold.

Walk with Me. Can you see the storm coming?
> It is dark and flashes with lightning.

Do you know how to get to the other side?
> Walk as I lead you and you cannot be harmed.

Pursue My love and hold onto peace; then joy will be within,
> Knowing I have come to free the slaves of sin.

Bringing forth My heaven is a task for all who love,
> For the measure I bring is the measure of the dove.

September 29

Message for a Young Woman

Hello, My daughter. I am with you in Spirit and Truth.

> *"God is Spirit, and those who worship Him must worship in spirit and truth." (John 4:24 NKJV)*

You are not alone. I see you. I am the Lord God Almighty, maker of heaven and earth. I will reveal Myself to you in many new ways. I am changing you from the inside out. I am beckoning you to seek after Me with diligence so I can reward you with much new discovery. Watch and see how I will use your willingness.

There are many false teachers in the world.

> *"But there were also false prophets among the people, even as there will be false teachers among you, who will secretly bring in destructive heresies, even denying the Lord who bought them, and bring on themselves swift destruction." (2 Peter 2:1 NKJV)*

Let me introduce you to the truth of My Son so you lack no good thing. I will lavish you with increasing awareness of My presence until your destiny is fully experienced. I will take your hand and lead you every time you call to Me. I am the Alpha and Omega, the beginning and the end, the first and the last *(Revelation 22:13)*.

There is nothing made that I did not make. In the same way, I will speak into existence many things you have not seen, and they shall come to pass in the name of My precious Son, Jesus.

Receive the fullness of My Holy Spirit and be increasingly filled with love, joy, and peace until your walk becomes effortless and your renewed faith can be as contagious as a fire of all that purifies. I am your redemption. Seek Me and receive the reward of your inheritance.

> *"Then I remembered the word of the Lord, how He said, 'John indeed baptized with water, but you shall be baptized with the Holy Spirit.'" (Acts 11:16 NKJV)*

October 2012

October 10

New Direction

Good morning, beloved! I would like you to consider what I say to be your new direction. Seek Me with all your heart and I will direct its passions so that every person is strongly suited for their area of focus. When I fill your cup, let it run over with gladness and remember My promise to never leave you. I alone am your supply. I alone am your portion.

Don't Open the Door to the Stranger

The stranger will try to gain access to your house. When he knocks, do not answer. Mountain climbing can be more difficult if you wish you were on a different mountain, so claim the land and occupy it! Why do people fail in ministry? One reason is a lack of planning. So, then, I need you to get organized, and I will guide your plans as I reveal them to you. You will need to be the overseer of emails so you can protect the email list from outside agendas.

Be Single-Minded

Not everyone will have the same level of understanding I have given. Be patient to develop people, but be on guard for divisional hearts. Division is born in duplicity. This is why there must be single-mindedness to the mind of Christ.

> *"Let this mind be in you which was also in Christ Jesus." (Philippians 2:5 NKJV)*

Renewal in the Word of God is what brings the mind of Christ. You are a pillar in My house and I am a rescuer of the wayward.

October 12 – The Law

Keep My Laws

I want my laws kept! To keep My commands means more than following My written word. It also means following My voice commands. Many follow My written word only and practice lawlessness by not hearing Me. This is caused by the sin of unbelief.

> *"Now He did not do many mighty works there because of their unbelief." (Matthew 13:58 NKJV)*

Misuse of Spiritual Gifts

Overcompensation is rampant in My church today. Misuse of My assigned spiritual gifts has taught many not to open the toolbox, although it's not the tool's fault, nor is it the designer's fault. I want My spiritual gifts taken out of the box-of-limitation and I, the Lord God Almighty, want to empower My children with My Spirit, which many have not yet received.

> *"There are diversities of gifts, but the same Spirit. There are differences of ministries, but the same Lord. And there are diversities of activities, but it is the same God who works all in all. But the manifestation of the Spirit is given to each one*

> *for the profit of all: for to one is given the word of wisdom through the Spirit, to another the word of knowledge through the same Spirit, to another faith by the same Spirit, to another gifts of healings by the same Spirit, to another the working of miracles, to another prophecy, to another discerning of spirits, to another different kinds of tongues, to another the interpretation of tongues. But one and the same Spirit works all these things, distributing to each one individually as He wills." (1 Corinthians 12:4-11 NKJV)*

Anyone who knowingly stands in the way of My Spirit will be removed, for I am second to none. I am the first and the last, the Alpha and the Omega, the Beginning and the End. I will not be mocked, nor will My army be directed by the wayward.

> *"I am the Alpha and the Omega, the Beginning and the End,' says the Lord, 'who is and who was and who is to come, the Almighty.'" (Revelation 1:8 NKJV)*

> *"Do not be deceived, God is not mocked; for whatever a man sows, that he will also reap." (Galatians 6:7 NKJV)*

Blocked Ears

To keep My commands is impossible without having the ability to hear. Because if I say it, how can one obey it unless they hear what I say? If I command you to go, how will you obey unless you hear Me?

> *"Your ears shall hear a word behind you, saying, 'This is the way, walk in it,' whenever you turn to the right hand or whenever you turn to the left." (Isaiah 30:21 NKJV)*

> *"For the hearts of this people have grown dull. Their ears are hard of hearing, and their eyes they have closed, lest they should see with their eyes and hear with their ears, lest they should understand with their hearts and turn, so that I should*

heal them. But blessed are your eyes for they see and your ears for they hear." (Matthew 13:15-16 NKJV)

"Then the righteous will shine forth as the sun in the Kingdom of their Father. He who has ears to hear, let him hear." (Matthew 13:43 NKJV)

"Having eyes, do you not see? And having ears, do you not hear? And do you not remember?" (Mark 8:18 NKJV)

This is why I have given you the call, beloved, to activate the ears of My sheep who do not know they were meant to hear. Blocked ears can be dangerous for Christians who do not hear My warning. Ear blockers are these—all of which are evil spirits that gain access through sin *(The antidote is in parenthesis.)*:

- Unbelief *(belief)*
- Pride *(humility)*
- Unworthiness *(worthiness)*
- Insecurity *(security)*
- Fear *(faith)*
- Laziness *(diligence)*, and
- Doubt *(assurance)*.

Empowered Living

If you believe you have been made worthy, you will be humble knowing that you did nothing to achieve it, and this knowledge will bring assurance of faith and security in your diligence. I am a rewarder of those who diligently seek Me and I, your heavenly Father, have approved of you through My Son, Jesus.

"But without faith it is impossible to please Him, for he who comes to God must believe that He is, and that He is a

rewarder of those who diligently seek Him." (Hebrews 11:6 NKJV)

If you could justify yourself through the requirements and satisfy the need to keep the law on your own, why would I have sent My Son, Jesus?

> *"Where is boasting then? It is excluded. By what law? Of works? No, but by the law of faith. Therefore we conclude that a man is justified by faith apart from the deeds of the law. Or is He the God of the Jews only? Is he not also the God of the Gentiles? Yes, of the Gentiles also." (Romans 3:27-29 NKJV)*

Jesus was the example of empowered living, so ask yourself if you have been empowered by My Spirit. Is it evidenced by your ability to obey My written commands through self-effort?

> *"So Jesus said to them again, 'Peace to you! As the Father has sent Me, I also send you.' And when He had said this, He breathed on them, and said to them, 'Receive the Holy Spirit. If you forgive the sins of any, they are forgiven them; if you retain the sins of any, they are retained.'" (John 20:21-23 NKJV)*

The Truth About Keeping the Law

I tell you the truth; My law cannot be kept by the flesh—only by My Spirit. Many believe they are righteous from their own doing or they, in self-deception, learn to quote Scripture as if knowing about Me is the same as knowing Me. I tell you the truth; unless you know the truth you don't know Me, but if you know the truth, then you will know Me, since it is I—the Truth. By knowing Me you will be free, and whom I, the Son, set free, they are free indeed.

> *"And you shall know the truth, and the truth shall make you free." (John 8:32 NKJV)*

> *"And I will pray the Father and He will give you another Helper, that He may abide with you forever—the Spirit of Truth, whom the world cannot receive, because it neither sees Him nor knows Him; but you know Him, for He dwells with you and will be in you." (John 14:16-17 NKJV)*

Image

My Spirit's mysteries are not revealed to the mind of the Pharisee who is still stuck in works of self-effort and pious religious ritual to be seen by men. Image is mine when you are in Me and I am in you. You were created in the image of God.

> *"So God created man in His own image; in the image of God He created him; male and female He created them." (Genesis 1:27 NKJV)*

When you are more concerned about how you appear to others than obedience to Me, you have entered into vanity. Lay down your idols of self-centeredness, My children, and pursue My will alone so that you will not stumble in the darkness of your own shadow, and step into the light that has come to show you the way.

Abundance

If you judge My messenger harshly and do not glean My truth, what would it profit you? But if you hear Me and let Him share with you My life, then surely you will have its abundance. Do I not wish to prosper your soul in every way? Learn then to listen and learn now to obey. A cup should be clean on the inside, not just on the outside. Then, with a clean heart to serve Me, your God alone, you will no longer live among the tombs of your past with dead man's bones and white-washed sepulchers. Be salt to cause thirst and be light to expose darkness, as I have done for you, both here and now and forevermore. I am!

"You are the salt of the earth; but if the salt loses its flavor, how shall it be seasoned? It is then good for nothing but to be thrown out and trampled underfoot by men." (Matthew 5:13 NKJV)

October 13

A Journey

I want to take you on a journey—this is a journey of the will:
   Will you to go?
      Will you to follow?
         Will you to trust?
           Will you to obey?
Hold out your hands.

Your will is like the wind,
   Shifting and changing around winding sins.
Holding the wheel, I take from your hands
   What fills up My heart; what scarred My two hands.
My feet only walk where My Father sends;
   All else would be wasted when I got to the end.
The road set high like My life from above,

    Up high on the cliffs as white as the dove;
Bringing forth peace on the wings of My sky;
    You know it's the voice of El Shaddai!
Lifting the fleeting, I rescue the weak.
    I long to spend time with My childlike sheep.
My voice, like a whisper, like the rustle of leaves,
    Brings a heart's willingness to the floor on its knees.
Patience will wait till My perfect time
    For the very best outcome is crafted by Mine.
My workers know how to be one with My Spirit
    Knowing the good they soon will inherit.

October 15 – To a Worship Leader

I AM

I AM is listening. Are you hearing Him?

I AM is My name. My answer is the same no matter what the problem.

I AM!

I am the reason.

I am the focus.

I am the breakthrough. When you know Me, you know

I AM, even when you are weak,

I am making you strong, and

I am not waiting for you to be perfect.

I am stabilizing your spiritual legs to carry a great deal of weight, but

I am with you so that you don't carry it alone because

I AM.

Here's what I am:

  Your strength,

    Your courage,

      Your life,

        Your hope,

          Your joy,

            Your provision,

              Your council,

              Your peace,

            Your measure,

            Your abundance,

          Your grace,

          Your approval,

        Your answer,

      Your light,

        Your wisdom,

          Your assurance,

            Your vision, and even your rest.

              Your question is My answer—I AM!

The Best Soil

Now that you understand, keep Me in your first thoughts so they become your first fruits that I can crack open to replant the seeds. Trees do not grow deep and wide without proper soil. So here is the best soil for planting:

Soil that has not become hardened and that has been churned up.

Soil that is not guarded from My rain and light.

Soil that has been tended to by removing the weeds or anything that could choke out new life.

Soil that has been fertilized, causing it to respond quickly, and

Soil that can withstand the erosion of this world.

October 17

Lord, I am here. What would you have me do tonight, Lord?

An Assignment

I want you to put someone else in charge of your scheduled meeting. Invite some to come with you to join the group meeting at Lighthouse. There is no competition between your groups. By coming in this way, you will show this to be true.

There is a woman I will bring to you with a cover upon her head. She will give you a message, and I will bring, through her, an unexpected blessing. Be mindful of what I have promised and remember that My voice is your safety. I will not be mocked. Sow well. Reap well. Sow life, unity, desire, and obedience. Care for all in love and kindness, believing for what has not yet come to pass.

You have my life, Lord. Use me as you choose.

Maturity Is Not Easy

Thank you, beloved. I hear your prayers, and I can see you are struggling, and again, I make you strong. It is My desire that you become fully developed. Maturity is not always easy. The process brings testing, and testing brings opportunity for advancement. I want you to be fully enabled. I want you to be mindful of My presence with you always. I desire to give you the full manifestation of My abiding presence.

This is how it will happen:

1. Be mindful that I am with you always, even unto the ends of the earth. If you know I am with you, you will not be afraid and your thoughts will become more easily directed.

2. Be willing to soak in My presence so you become overtaken by My Spirit so it is no longer you who lives but Me who lives in you.

3. Give away the revelation so I can fill you up fresh and new.

4. Know there is no shortage in My heaven, and I can pour through you My River of Life.

5. My gifts will never be taken from you. They are irrevocable!

October 21 – The Heart

The Lord gave me these words like I was actually speaking them for a message to the people at The Rock of the Harbor church (now Rock Revival Center).

The Heart Matters

We know our heart is right when we no longer speak or sing to be heard, but so that Christ can be exalted alone. We know our heart is right when the things we treasure most are eternal—then we are becoming heaven-minded and Christ-focused. Remember that where your treasure is, there your heart will be also.

> *"For where your treasure is, there your heart will be also."* (Matthew 6:21 and Luke 12:34 NKJV)

If we analyze how we spend our time and money, we will see where our heart really is. We will invest in what we believe in. We will spend our time where we have placed our hope. Where is your heart? Is it here in the fallen world or in the Kingdom of God assigned to save it? Is your heart set to glorify the appetite of self? Is your heart soft and moldable, or hard and stubborn?

Now the Lord changes His words to read in the first person:

Good and Evil

The heart is the instrument I use to pour My Holy Spirit from. It contains a mixture of good and evil. Some say to "follow your heart," although My word says the heart is deceitful and wicked; who can know it?

> *"The heart is deceitful above all things, and desperately wicked; who can know it?" (Jeremiah 17:9 NKJV)*

On the other hand, it has the capacity to display loving kindness, grace, and mercy when balanced in submission to My Holy Spirit. Without the right heart, it is impossible to have harmony. A surrendered heart becomes renewed and restored, one that can be used as My instrument.

A Hardened Heart

My melodies are meant to break down the hard-hearted and bring back sensitivity to those emotions that have been shut down by hazardous living. Drugs, alcohol, food, and even irresponsibility have become an escape for many of My children who do not know they were meant to feel and respond, according to My Spirit, through a restored heart and a renewed mind.

> *"Put off, concerning your former conduct, the old man which grows corrupt according to the deceitful lusts, and be renewed in the spirit of your mind." (Ephesians 4:22-23 NKJV)*

Choices can be fun, but if a person chooses, based on fear or woundedness, then often the wrong choice is made. When choices are made with a right heart, motivated by the right Spirit through the renewed mind, a natural progression is made toward success. When lessons are not learned and adjustments are not made, a hazard occurs.

Fresh Bread

I want to light up your path and resurrect your understanding with Fresh Bread that is My word, consumed by you, My children, who are rewarded with My life when you come to Me, hungry.

> *"And Jesus said to them, 'I am the bread of life. He who comes to Me shall never hunger, and he who believes in Me shall never thirst.'" (John 6:35 NKJV)*

Feed on My truth until it fills you, and I will become your satisfaction so you do not settle for any substitute that could dilute your experience in My fullness.

Birthright

A birthright means more than the "right to be born," but the right to be born again into new life.

> *"Jesus answered and said to him, 'Most assuredly, I say to you, unless one is born again, he cannot see the Kingdom of God.'" (John 3:3 NKJV)*

> *"If you confess with your mouth the Lord Jesus and believe in your heart that God has raised Him from the dead, you will be saved." (Romans 10:8-9 NKJV)*

It is no longer you who live but I, your Savior, who lives in you.

> *"I have been crucified with Christ; it is no longer I who live, but Christ lives in me; and the life which I now live in the flesh I live by faith in the Son of God, who loved me and gave Himself for me." (Galatians 2:20 NKJV)*

So let your deeds reflect your understanding to walk out your faith so those who see a pure heart will praise Me, your Lord.

Action Is Proof

The heart is a holding tank; it has a tendency to remember the pains of life; it remembers and stores trauma. A healthy heart will be constantly cleansed until I have given to it My ambitions.

    Is your heart right before Me?

    Is it focused on what My will is?

    Is it more interested in My purpose than its own?

The test is what proves the answer—*your action* is the proof! The heart that is healthy will take the right action. Thoughts do become actions. From the mouth the heart speaks.

> *"A good man out of the good treasure of his heart brings forth good; and an evil man out of the evil treasure of his heart brings forth evil. For out of the abundance of the heart his mouth speaks." (Luke 6:5 NKJV)*

This is why responding to life with the Word of God is so important for living a long and healthy life. A wounded soul can bog down the heart and so can the unconditioned body. Every walk begins with a commitment, and a desire to fulfill is worthless if there is no action that is committed to a direction. I will always bring blessing to reward action because My Kingdom is not for spectators. My Kingdom's rewards are given to participants.

October 21

It's NOT About

IT'S NOT ABOUT a particular church—

    It's about a Kingdom.

IT'S NOT ABOUT our singing—

    It's about why we sing.

IT'S NOT ABOUT what's in it for us—

    It's about what we bring to others.

IT'S NOT ABOUT fulfilling our ambition—

    It's about pleasing the one who fills us with His.

IT'S NOT ABOUT who we are—

    It's about who He is.

IT'S NOT ABOUT what we've done—

    It's about what He's allowed us to do.

IT'S NOT ABOUT how we can fit in—

    It's about where He places us to fit.

IT'S NOT ABOUT this world at all—

    It's about His Kingdom coming to save it.

IT'S NOT ABOUT our limits—

    It's about Him who has no limits.

IT'S NOT ABOUT what has not yet happened—

    It's about everything that has.

October 22 – Finances

Money Is a Tool

To be highly effective, you will need to change the way you think about money. Money is a tool. It can be useful. My systems are different than the systems of this world. I want you to learn to operate on a budget. If it's not within the budget, then you don't do it. If it's not planned or if it's over a certain predetermined amount, you don't spend it!

Crack Down on Your Money

Justification is like punching holes in the bottom of your financial boat. The more you justify your spending, the faster you sink in despair. It's time you direct your money instead of allowing your money to direct you. You have been at the end of the whip, and I want you holding it by the handle. Crack down on your money! It's meant to work for you—not you for it! I have a storehouse of plenty, and I pour it out on those who steward what they have been given, whether great or small. I know it can seem hard, but it doesn't matter how little or how much; the same principles apply. It's time to get your house in order.

Discipline Is Part of Discipleship

I want you to open an account with a credit union and set up your allowances. Remember that a lot of small spending is like having a lot of small holes in the bottom of your boat. Enough small holes equal one big hole that can sink your progress. You will have to be strict and exercise much more discipline, a very necessary part of discipleship. Just remember that without discipline, your ship sinks and there are no disciples left to see you reach the other side.

Leadership is founded on sound principles proven to work. I can see your struggle, and it is time your struggle ends in victory. It's hopeless when you continue in the same patterns of defeat. What will restore your hope is success. Do what I am asking. Keep a check registry with you so you know exactly what you have at all times. Do not rely on a bank's faulty system to tell you. You have seen the tricks to rob you with unnecessary fees. The system takes advantage of people who do not have their house in order.

Wants vs. Needs

Be at peace, for I am upon you in word and truth. When you owe someone money, then spend on extras, you are taking away what is not yours to take. When you spend money that belongs to another, you are stealing. Be sure you do not unknowingly rob Me or others.

> *"Will a man rob God? Yet you have robbed Me! But you say, 'In what way have we robbed you?' In tithes and offerings. You are cursed with a curse, for you have robbed Me, even this whole nation." (Malachi 3:8-9 NKJV)*

I understand that you have certain needs. But many things you say you need are only wants. Be careful not to see wants as needs. This is another trick the attacker of your finances uses to keep you poor.

October 23

An Open Rebuke

Sharpen your skills and learn to embrace your destiny by giving Me place to move through you as I have previously intended. You are who I say you are, not what the world says or even thinks. I will bring glory and honor to those who bring glory and honor to Me. The run-off will be a gushing forth of My open gates and the blessings will not be contained. Wicked hearts will be purged and tested until I have accomplished My goal of refinement. I will not allow for improper order in My house of hope. Pride will not stand in My house, and I will not exalt the proud.

> *"But He gives more grace. Therefore He says: 'God resists the proud, but gives grace to the humble.'" (James 4:6 NKJV)*

> *"Pride goes before destruction, and a haughty spirit before a fall." (Proverbs 16:18 NKJV)*

Many believe you are a lone ranger; this is how they justify not partnering with you. Some of those whom I have called are in rebellion, operating out of their own pride. I have purposely held back the wrong hearts so as not to spoil the spawn. I am elevating pure hearts and those who have enough humility to serve in deed—not in empty words.

October 24

I am selling meat door to door, even though I am a pastor of a church.

Rest in Your Work

Rest in My love. Don't wrestle within yourself. Results come from resting in your work. To rest in your work, you need to allow yourself to rest in the peace that comes from My presence within you. I will help you sell the meat if you will only go to the doors I lead you to and say only what I give you to say. You waste a lot of time knocking on the wrong doors, even though you know I can lead you to the right places by My Spirit. Some places I lead you to are opportunities for prayer, and some are opportunities for provision, and some for both. You have overcome much fear, but I am helping you to overcome all fear so you can walk in reverence of Me at all times, protected by your faith in My finished work at the cross.

October 25

Lord, your servant is listening…

The Sweet Spot

I want you to remain in the sweet spot of your faith. Give Me your attention like this and I will fill your thoughts with mine. The renewed mind of Christ comes to those who seek it from a heart of surrender.

> *"For who has known the mind of the Lord that he may instruct Him? But we have the mind of Christ." (1 Corinthians 2:16 NKJV)*

My words of truth bring a balance to your understanding so that lies are plucked from the soil of your mind. Your heart is the garden I've been tending. Can you feel My Spirit upon you? Do you sense My surrounding presence? My Spirit will be expanding around you because I have prepared it to abide with you, in power and truth, to shed the shackles of what has brought slaves into the dungeon of self-focus. Be mindful of My peace as it blankets your soul, and find what I have prepared for you. As you proclaim its acknowledgment, I will make your path straight. Minister to My people, beloved. Lavish them with Agape love.[7]

---

[7] Agape is a Greek word used in the New Testament meaning the fatherly love of God for humans as well as the human reciprocal love for God. In Scripture, the transcendent Agape love is the highest form of love and is contrasted with Eros or Erotic love, and Philia, or brotherly love.

October 26

Here I am, Lord. You have my attention!

A Tip

Do not waste time trying to help people who do not want your help. Just pray that My truth will liberate them.

I Still Discipline Those I Love

When I call you to come, you hear Me and I bring you into My inner chamber where the Beast has no access to you. I will adjust your adversaries, and those who rise against you, in word or deed, will be put down under your feet. I am your protection, provision, and strong tower of refuge.

> *"The name of the Lord is a strong tower; the righteous run to it and are safe." (Proverbs 18:10 NKJV)*

Live in Me as I live in you so no weapon formed against you can prosper.

> *"No weapon formed against you shall prosper, and every tongue which rises against you in judgment you shall condemn. This is the heritage of the servants of the L*ORD*, and their*

righteousness is from Me,' says the LORD.*" (Isaiah 54:17 NKJV)*

Rebellion against My plan cannot be left unquestioned by My righteous judgment. I am the defender and My heart is just. I do see through the finished work at the cross; however, I am just. I still discipline those I love and chasten those I call My own. Some come quickly through My fire of refinement, and some walk through and are destroyed by the disorientation of their own pride.

> *"Now no chastening seems to be joyful for the present, but painful; nevertheless, afterward it yields the peaceable fruit of righteousness to those who have been trained by it." (Hebrews 12:11 NKJV)*

A Gift of Service

If you bring to Me a gift of service, is it to seek a reward or to please Me out of love? The rewards are endless when a heart is postured in the humility of praise. Sending forth My message is not for the weak and faint, but for the bold and righteous. My words bring liberation and transformation to all who take heed. But many do not hear Me beyond the voice of their own desires. The secret is finding your desires in Me. Then your desires are lined up with mine.

Self-Reliance or God-Dependence

Many struggle from their own willfulness and never reach their destiny of greatness. Failure and success come from either self-reliance or God-dependence. God-dependence brings the sweetness of victory and the lasting savor of accomplishment. There is no lasting fulfillment in those who pursue themselves through self-reliance.

October 27

A Move of My Spirit

This equipping center is changing the way that church is done. It's no longer about developing a comfortable routine; it's about following the Holy Spirit and honoring God with the resources entrusted. I am calling forth a move of My Spirit, to reach the world of intellectual giants, who have been snared by their own brilliant minds and have become their own God—who stand as their own idol on the pedestal of their religion.

I am sorting and separating the people who will from those who will not—those who want My will and My Kingdom from those who do not. Those who chase their own will and attempt to build upon the foundations of man, from the flesh, are destined to fail. Watch and see what the Lord God Almighty is about to release and know that the fire cannot be contained. I will hold back the willful, while I bring forward and elevate the willing and surrendered saints who have said yes to My plans that are indeed made.

Can you feel My intensity toward you? Do you know what is welling up inside of your innermost being? It is the designer's plan, resounding within you to confirm My truth that there be no mistake about it!

I will elevate.

I will separate.

I will evaluate the heart.

You have passed through some fire and have kept your eyes on Me. There is so much to do, but I want it done through My rest. It is possible to be held in My deepness and become light and effective in My Holy Spirit's effortlessness.

> *"Come to Me, all you who labor and are heavy laden, and I will give you rest." (Matthew 11:28 NKJV)*

October 28

To My Praying Children

I am moving now according to your prayers, My children. One sends a thousand and two sends ten thousand.

> *"How could one chase a thousand, and two put ten thousand to flight, unless their Rock had sold them, and the Lord had surrendered them?" (Deuteronomy 32:30 NKJV)*

I have released My Spirit this morning, according to your prayers of selflessness. When you pray from victory, I release My great power to adjust what has departed from Me. My people are rising up as a mighty army to take back the ground that has been stolen. You have understood My grief as My heart pours from the deep places. Do not lose sight that the victory is won, that My work on the cross is the finished work.

> *"So when Jesus had received the sour wine, He said, 'It is finished!' And bowing His head, He gave up His spirit."* (John 19:30 NKJV)

Be-being filled with My Spirit, My warriors and you shall not fail, for My inheritance is being fully manifested upon you. Search your hearts and allow My peace so you do not become dismayed.

November 2012

November 1

Living Water

Living water is pouring from the Rock, and it will not stop gushing until the desert is emptied from its dryness. Many who are thirsty will come from far away and will drink and be filled as My purposes are fulfilled.

Abundant Life

Note My concerns for your progress and adjust those things quickly so I can overtake you with goodness and mercy.

> *"Surely goodness and mercy shall follow me all the days of my life; and I will dwell in the house of the Lord forever." (Psalm 23:6 NKJV)*

Surely you will not fail as you have fixed your eyes on Me. It's the dawn of a new era. Many in the world do not connect sin with punishment or consequences, but My natural laws are as solid as the air that gives life and the gravity that pulls down. They are set! It is My desire to show you the way so My truth can bring to you the flow of life. Abundant life is not lacking anything. It is limited only in perception.

> *"The thief does not come except to steal, and to kill, and to destroy. I have come that they may have life, and that they may have it more abundantly." (John 10:10 NKJV)*

Correction

Evil has festered against you as you have exposed the forces of darkness in another. I am a just and righteous judge, and there is no limit to My love, but that love includes correction. I will not ignore My right to discipline those I love and to chasten those members of My royal family in order to break strongholds and crush the head of the serpent that schemes in the shadows, plotting to plunder My purpose.

> *"For whom the Lord loves He chastens, and scourges every son whom He receives." (Hebrews 12:6 NKJV)*

> *"For the weapons of our warfare are not carnal but mighty in God for pulling down strongholds." (2 Corinthians 10:4 NKJV)*

Will You?

Will you become what I have called you to be and accept responsibility for My complete favor? Will you enter My inner court and dine with Me? Will you go to the church on the hill and show support to the leaders there? Do not speak of your own work and I will carry out My purpose in sending you. I am your refuge. Hide in the cleft of My Rock where the safety is and you will be sheltered by My Spirit and Truth until the storm passes.

November 2

A Mighty Army

It is good to see and hear what My voice is saying. Water is gushing from the Rock and, like salmon are strengthened by rushing the current, so it will be for those who continue in moving beyond resistance. Purpose yourself to fight the currents as you deposit the seed. That is My holy ambition for you as you die to self and arrive at your birthright. I will raise up a mighty army from your willing service and they will become Holy Spirit driven with My armor intact to:

Tear down, and

Root out, and

Bring to life that which was lost and broken.

Child Likeness

Splashing in the water encourages playfulness and children do not need help entering into it. Only those who grow out of it must learn to put off their childish ways while entering into child-likeness.

> *"Assuredly, I say to you, unless you are converted and become as little children, you will by no means enter the Kingdom of heaven."* (Matthew 18:3 NKJV)

Rivers find the outlet to release without instruction. So it is with willingness to pour out—you find a place that receives you. Jumping on sand, your footprint leaves an impression. I am guiding you to the places where that impression will remain.

A Rhyme with a Message

The beach is fun while in the sun, but many are cold in the dark.

> So, bring the light and joyful song until the clouds depart.

Depressed, some cover the truth as if it's meant to be,

> That every voice should hold it in, not speak to set men free.

I have asked to be acknowledged in everything you do

> So I can guide you through the storms, bringing heaven down to you.

Your food is here, your daily bread, so gather truth and eat!

> Then give away what you have found and teach the sheep to pray.

Prayers should change when you realize the victory that is won;

> For I have called, you have come, and I grafted you a son.

Sonship, kingship, priestly royal blood sincere,

> Has brought you to the breakthrough for I knew the year.

I have gone before you to plan your Kingdom play,

> And this is the time, My Kingdom hour, to teach you how to pray.

You went last night to the church on the hill and asked the people there

> To stretch their faith and open up; they gasped for more fresh air.

You spoke My truth and released My peace and many came to see

> That I have called them back to intimacy with Me.

Like drawing down your pail into My holy pool,

> I bring you to My varsity—Heaven's State University School!

Press into Me as I surround you even more, and

> Watch Me by My Spirit open every door.

Be mindful of My presence, giving you its gift

> To help in teaching others—not to let them drift.

Pile wood together and you'll have a brighter flame,

> Hotter than before, now free of guilt and shame.

November 9 – Intimacy, Part 1

God's Sons

Sunday's theme, as you have suspected, is "Intimacy with God." I am God's Son and you, through Me, are also His son—so then, your inheritance is mine and My inheritance is yours.

> "Blessed be the God and Father of our Lord Jesus Christ, who according to his abundant mercy has begotten us again to a living hope through the resurrection of Jesus Christ from the dead, to an inheritance incorruptible and undefiled and that does not fade away, reserved in heaven for you, who are kept by the power of God through faith for salvation ready to be revealed in the last time." (1 Peter 1:3-5 NKJV)

The royal priesthood was not reserved for Me, Jesus, but for all who have been given the right to be called sons and daughters.

> "But you are a chosen generation, a royal priesthood, a holy nation, his own special people, that you may proclaim the praises of Him who called you out of darkness into His marvelous light; who once were not a people but are now the people of God, who had not obtained mercy but now have obtained mercy." (1 Peter 2:9-10 NKJV)

Share the Secrets

I will renew the minds of those who will call on Me from intimacy. To know about something does not mean you have experienced it. Many know about Me but do not have a close relationship with Me. Many do not know how to have a close relationship, but I can show you, beloved, how to share the secrets that are not meant to be kept—the secrets that Satan does not want My people to know about.

Time

Intimacy starts with time. You cannot become intimate with someone you never spend time with. That would be impossible. The way time is spent leaves an impression of what one values. Anyone can say they love Me above all else, but what I see is actual. I know the heart condition of all My children, and I can see love expressed for Me through the investment of time. Intimacy is developed in time deposits. Time can be spent on:

- Sitting in My presence.
- Reading My words.
- Receiving My words through instructional revelation.
- Becoming mindful of My presence during the tasks of the day.

Fear of Intimacy

Many fear intimacy with Me because of:

Guilt,

Shame,

Condemnation,

Unworthiness, or

Pride.

Guilt says you shouldn't go to God—look at what you've done. Condemnation says you should hide from God because He is angry at you for what you've done and is about to punish you because you deserve to be punished. Remember when you did this or that terrible thing? This leads to a feeling of unworthiness and insecurity, which brings pride, posing as a "false protection," which leads to the desire to convince everyone you have value.

Made Worthy

If you become intimate with Me, you will become secure and receive My:

Comfort,

Assurance,

Affirmation, and

Love.

When this happens, you will realize you have been made worthy by justification at the cross so that your motivation is now selfless fulfillment of your destiny in Me instead of selfish-ambition and self-focus. Intimacy is a secret weapon against the destroyer who tries to convince My children I am against them when really I am for them.

A Snare

When the Enemy convinces someone I am against them, this can become a snare that triggers someone to be against Me, opening them up to become an antichrist, which is also a spirit. Many who serve Me have fallen away in their hearts and have exchanged their intimacy for power, money, and fame, which are lures from the Devil. If my people get drawn into serving these tempting lures, they can easily become ineffective and more dangerous yet—a discredit to My Kingdom.

> *"And a servant of the Lord must not quarrel but be gentle to all, able to teach, patient, in humility correcting those who are in opposition, if God perhaps will grant them repentance, so that they may know the truth, and that they may come to their senses and escape the snare of the devil, having been taken captive by him to do his will." (2 Timothy 2:24-26 NKJV)*

A Protection

Intimacy protects My Kingdom, and My will is to draw all My children into its protection. True unity or oneness can only happen when there is true intimacy. My peace is a blessing released upon those who walk in intimacy with Me. My favor is a blessing upon those who value My will above their own, which is displayed by obedience.

> *"I can of Myself do nothing. As I hear, I judge; and My judgement is righteous, because I do not seek My own will but the will of the Father who sent Me." (John 5:30 NKJV)*

Love and Obedience

Love obeys. If there is no obedience, there is no love.

> *"If you love me, keep My commandments." (John 14:15 NKJV)*

Love is the most important part of growing intimate, and love must be demonstrated in action—not words alone—to be genuine. I know if someone really loves Me because they do what I say with their time and their money. My resources are endless, and they are released with precision on those who are intimate.

Intimacy demands obedience, for obedience cannot exist without intimacy. Intimacy will become your greatest investment, and those who discover its treasure will inherit their birthright from My Kingdom. Seek first the Kingdom of God and His righteousness and all will be added.

> *"But seek first the Kingdom of God and His righteousness, and all these things shall be added to you."* (Matthew 6:33 NKJV)

Seeking Me brings intimacy that releases My Kingdom, so I say to you—seek Me and you will find Me when you seek Me with all your heart.

> *"And you will seek Me and find Me, when you search for Me with all your heart."* (Jeremiah 29:13 NKJV)

Where Is Your Treasure?

Remember that where your treasure is, there your heart will be also.

> *"For where your treasure is, there your heart will be also."* (Matthew 6:21 NKJV)

So, ask yourself honestly, "What do you treasure?" Then track your time and your spending to see if it matches and you will know if an adjustment is needed for Me to have your whole heart. If you say you love Me but you do not show it, then surely you do not love Me but yourself alone. If you love Me, you will give Me the first fruits of your time as well as your tithes and offerings. Sin breaks down intimacy.

I Desire Intimacy

Intimacy is what I desire most, just as those of you who are parents would also desire the same from your own children. What would be the point of having children, only to be ignored by them? So then, know Me and show Me that you know Me by growing intimate with the one who has called you to intimacy, even now in the darkness of this world, to become a light that can only shine bright if you charge up in Me. Once you are filled with the light of My truth, you can fill others. I am a jealous God, and I do not want to compete, so then acknowledge Me in all your ways and I will make your paths straight and full of the light that shines back on the one who made it.

> *"In all your ways acknowledge Him, and He shall direct your paths." (Proverbs 3:6 NKJV)*

I am He—the Alpha and Omega, the beginning and the end—the designer of time, and you, beloved, are My investment. The best return is your intimacy!

November 10 – Intimacy, Part 2

Seek Me

Intimacy is a secret ingredient to supernatural success. Seek Me and you still find Me when you seek Me with **ALL** your heart. That is another secret ingredient—emphasis on ALL.

> *"And you will seek Me and find Me, when you search for Me with all your heart." (Jeremiah 29:13 NKJV)*

My secrets are not revealed to those who are playing both sides.

> *"But let him ask in faith, with no doubting, for he who doubts is like a wave of the sea, driven and tossed by the wind. For let not that man suppose that he will receive anything from the Lord; he is a double-minded man, unstable in all his ways." (James 1:6-8 NKJV)*

My secrets are meant to be revealed, uncovered, and brought to the surface like gold, but far more valuable. I love to lavish those who will come to Me with the right heart. When I see that a heart is committed to Me wholly, I deposit into it every good and perfect gift so that an overflow can pour forth like a rushing river, flooding the thirsty to lead them out of the desert.

> *"Every good gift and every perfect gift is from above, and comes down from the Father of lights, with whom there is no variation or shadow of turning."* (James 1:17 NKJV)

Drive Out Rebellion

Rebellion must be driven out for intimacy to thrive. Then you can receive the full measure of My promise. Fear of intimacy is caused by a wounded soul. This is why My love must be received fully to fully be fulfilled in intimacy.

Reward of Intimacy

People intimidated by intimacy must press beyond it to receive its prize and become lavished by My love's measure. For it to be fully received, one must seek Me wholeheartedly—then I will bring forth the unreserved measure I have longed to release upon My hungry and thirsty children. Do not be intimidated by intimacy, but come to Me just as you are, My blessed people, so I can lavish you with the reward of intimacy; then you will be able to receive the full measure of My Agape love, which will never run dry nor become depleted, but will pour forth as a raging river from the Rock that is your salvation. There I have called you to stand!

> *"The LORD lives! Blessed be my Rock! Let God be exalted, The Rock of my salvation!"* (2 Samuel 22:47 NKJV)

> *"He only is my Rock and my salvation; He is my defense; I shall not be greatly moved."* (Psalm 62:2 NKJV)

November 18 – Faith

Faith Fed by Action

Faith has substance to sustain you.

Faith is expansive when it is fed by action.

Faith does. If it does not do, it is not faith.

Faith is the only way to please Me.

Faith does not hide, but steps out no matter how hard it is.

Faith delivers reward. Reward is substance, just as

Faith is the substance of things hoped for and the evidence of things not yet seen.

> *"Now faith is the substance of things hoped for, the evidence of things not seen." (Hebrews 11:1 NKJV)*

If you believe, you will step out.

If you do not step out, you show lack of faith.

If you believe, you will always receive.

However, it does no good to believe without action because belief also takes action or it is not belief but unbelief, which counters faith.

> *"For as the body without the spirit is dead, so faith without works is dead also."* (James 2:26 NKJV)

Breakthrough

Facing fear by moving into action is stepping out in faith and faith can bring forth the supernatural reward called breakthrough. Breakthrough is a result of applying My word and walking into the action of doing what I say, not being a hearer only.

> *"But be doers of the word, and not hearers only, deceiving yourselves. For if anyone is a hearer of the word and not a doer, he is like a man observing his natural face in a mirror; for he observes himself, goes away, and immediately forgets what kind of man he was."* (James 1:22-24 NKJV)

If You Do

I know that you love Me, your God, if you do what I say. If you do not, I know that you do not love Me, nor do you believe or you would do. If you do not act upon what you hear, what good would it be to hear? Faith is:

Hearing My promise,

Believing it, and

Walking in action to receive what has been promised.

Many say, "I believe," but this is nothing more than double-mindedness.

> *"He is a double-minded man, unstable in all his ways."* (James 1:8 NKJV)

If you wish to be stable in all your ways, then show your faith by your deeds, but do not rely on your deeds alone, for they cannot save you. I am your Savior, and if you will hear My voice, you will be guided into amazing grace that will motivate your action, and this action is faith-filled to help you to be faithful.

Practice Obedience

Eat My words to enjoy their truth, gleaning every morsel, but always put them quickly into action, practicing obedience so your faith can materialize the substance of what you are hoping for.

> *"Your words were found, and I ate them, and your word was to me the joy and rejoicing of my heart; for I am called by Your name, O Lord God of hosts." (Jeremiah 15:16 NKJV)*

Do not forget, you are a co-laborer with Me, your God, so do not be as the hypocrite who says, "I'm just trusting the Lord" while he sits on the couch and eats his chips.

The Greatest Is Love

I reward faith in action. Faith without action is not faith at all.

   Hope is action;

     Love is action;

        Faith is action.

   The greatest of these is love, and

     Love believes by faith, and

        Faith is fueled by hope.

   And all of these will do,

     And will work,

        Or there will be an absence of them.

Exercise faith and hope and you will become amazing at loving others:

Believing in Me,

   Yourself, and

     Others.

Give Me a reason to increase in you by showing Me action. My hope is in your ability to believe, for I have given everyone a measure so that not one would have an excuse but all would be able to become a steward of what I have given.

Faith Dulled by Fear

Do not let your faith become dulled by fear.

> *"But He said to them, 'Why are you so fearful? How is it that you have no faith?'" (Mark 4:40 NKJV)*

Do not let your faith be diminished by the spirit of unbelief.

> *"So Jesus said to them, 'Because of your unbelief; for assuredly, I say to you, if you have faith as a mustard seed, you will say to this mountain, "Move from here to there," and it will move; and nothing will be impossible for you.'" (Matthew 17:20 NKJV)*

If you cannot get free of unbelief, fast and pray, for I, the Lord God Almighty, want you to be faith-filled and overflowing with My endless power and authority to move heaven on earth. This can only happen when:

You are filled with My life and power,

   Released by My word in action,

     According to your faith in action, that

Brings forth My unstoppable favor.

No excuses!

No exceptions!

No limitations!

Fill Up on Faith

Fill up on faith wherever it can be found, and consume it until it becomes your new way of life, for this is the greatest time in history to be full of faith—faith-filled, and faithful until all has been accomplished on earth as it is in heaven. Chase after her (faith) as wisdom and usher in My bride to join Her with the bridegroom to become a match made in heaven, My faithful warriors, whom I am now beside! *(Jesus is standing in the room but can only be seen by those who see by the Spirit.)*

November 21

I'm here, Lord, listening for You....

Pace Yourself

Pace yourself. Success is a series of tests and steps—not one burst of sudden exertion. Move with My Spirit as you move into My peace. The rest you will find is to stabilize your motivations.

> *"Let us therefore be diligent to enter that rest, lest anyone fall according to the same example of disobedience." (Hebrews 4:11 NKJV)*

You do not need to worry about every detail, trying to be perfect. Just do as I guide you, according to My Spirit within you. I have designed you to respond to Me in communion so that we can work closely together.

Full Surrender

Most of My followers have not yet found the freedom of total surrender, but because you have, I can much more easily direct you. Not surrendering all is like falling asleep at the wheel. You may be dreaming you are driving, but dreaming you are driving does not mean you are. If you are, then I'm not. If I am, then you are not. If I'm driving and you fall asleep, you are not in any danger, but if you are driving and you fall asleep, everyone who is your passenger can be put in danger.

Wake up, you sluggard, and swing your bat!

> *"The sluggard will not plow by reason of the cold; therefore shall he beg in harvest, and have nothing." (Proverbs 20:4 KJV)*

If you don't try, you most surely cannot win. I am going to guide you, and I am going to see to it that you have plenty of opportunities to glorify your God!

> *"I will instruct you and teach you in the way you should go; I will guide you with My eye." (Psalm 32:8 NKJV)*

November 23 – Building a Church

A Family

You will assemble a large family of believers to have the mind of Christ and to love one another as Christ loves the church. This church will grow and increase in numbers and will be organized, yet Holy Spirit led. The Holy Spirit will continue to give the agenda and will guide in giving breakthrough and breakout. I want you to realize the importance of having a non-typical service.

Elements of Success

Here are the elements of success: The right people in the right seats with the right attitude bring the right result. My Holy Spirit will pour out, ever increasing, as these components surface:

- Order yet freedom,
- Structure in obedience, and
- Oversight through servanthood.

Goal setting is important to developing a strong structure. Structure is as strong as its weakest link. Find and expose the weak areas and My Spirit can restore, with revelation and application, bringing transformation.

Make Strong Leaders

You must have strong leadership. Be willing to confront weakness for the purpose of making strong leaders. Berries must be picked when they are ripe. If picked too soon, they will be sour; if too late, they are mushy and not strongly firm. So it is with My servants. Let those who are strong serve when they are ready lest they become bitter from not being useful, and from their service, they will become solid. Sweetness is a result of gratefulness. A true servant is happy serving and takes joy in giving of themselves.

Elephants are very large land animals with huge ears, but they are not very intelligent. They could trample to death many things if they wanted to, but they are afraid of a mouse. Big ears do not mean great hearing, and large size and weight does not mean power and fearlessness. Do not judge from outer appearances but rather inward evidence shown through outward displays.

> *"For man looks at the outward appearance, but the Lord looks at the heart." (1 Samuel 16:7b NKJV)*

If you are a giraffe, don't take the advice of a turtle. The giraffe doesn't see what the turtle sees, and the turtle doesn't see what the giraffe sees.

Breathe

Breathe in to breathe out, and as you release, you will have capacity to be filled. Breathe in, My friend, and breathe out with wind that moves heaven with the voice that will shake faulty foundations. Blow on problems by speaking out My powerful truths and they will topple like a deck of cards. Cast down idols and free the captives of deception who in their arrogance do not believe they could be deceived.

Infrastructure

Infrastructure needs to be understood. Infrastructure is Sunday's topic, and the theme will promote participation. Use the example of LivingStone Lodge—your parents' building project. Once the logs were placed on the foundation, the infrastructure was in place, but everything else had to be added: the roof, the partitions, the flooring, the electrical components, the plumbing, the windows and doors, the closets and cupboards, etc. So it is with The Rock of the Harbor *(now The Rock Revival Center)*.

The areas that need to be studied are:

- Childcare
- Greeters
- Projection
- Signs
- Sound
- Announcements
- Preaching
- Follow-up
- Bulletins
- Worship

November 24 – My Church

The Foundation

The foundation of My church can only stand if it is built on My son, Jesus Christ—the Rock!

> *"According to the grace of God which was given to Me, as a wise master builder I have laid the foundation, and another builds on it. But let each one take heed how he builds on it. For no other foundation can anyone lay than that which is laid, which is Jesus Christ." (1 Corinthians 3:10-11 NKJV)*

Without the Rock, you have no foundation.

> *"The LORD lives! Blessed be My Rock! Let the God of my salvation be exalted." (Psalm 18:46 NKJV)*

> *"The LORD is my Rock and my fortress and my deliverer; my God, my strength, in whom I will trust; my shield and the horn of my salvation, my stronghold." (Psalm 18:2 NKJV)*

Many men have attempted to build upon idols, and in the end, they wallow in defeat. "On Christ, the solid Rock I stand; all other ground is sinking sand" is a favorite hymn in the heavens, and the supernatural is witnessed by those who put their trust in Me.

Unstable Ground

People do not want to walk where the ground is unstable, but rather, where they know it will not give way. If you detect the ground is uncertain, you will most likely avoid it, walk around it, and look to see if anyone is falling. I want you, My people, to focus on Me—the Rock of your Salvation, so you will know precisely where to stand. Then you can become maximized in your willingness to serve My purpose.

Great Leaders

Great leaders are *not* born—they are developed, and I am the developer of all those who submit to My process. Many give Me just a part of themselves, so that is the part I develop. I can only develop the parts given to Me—so give Me all of you, even if only in stages, and I will shape and mold My masterpiece so it can be displayed as a model for My glory, says the Lord.

Broaden Your Horizons

It's time to broaden your horizons and to give yourselves to Me completely as I lift you up above your circumstance that is shifty and short-lived. Wayward action is the result of wayward thinking. This is why you must allow Me to renew your minds with the word—My Bible.

> *"And do not be conformed to this world, but be transformed by the renewing of your mind, that you may prove what is that good and acceptable and perfect will of God." (Romans 12:2 NKJV)*

Self-Check

1. Is your every decision based on My truth?

2. Is your every ambition according to My plan?

3. Is your every step taken according to My purpose so that you desire to do My will?

Why not?

Excuses are like sinking sand.

Procrastination from laziness is like sinking sand.

Lies toward yourself or others are like sinking sand.

The truth is the Rock, JESUS!

November 30 – Evangelism

Purification

When my truth is planted in the heart of a hearer, it is as a flame. My Holy Spirit is as a breath blowing to kindle what has begun. Souls that burn for truth with passion are easily ignited by My spoken words. Being on fire for Me means more than to submit to purification, it also means to become increasingly contagious. Words are as logs, and logs are what increase the flames of My passion for souls. The Lord your God is as a consuming fire—not to destroy, but to spread My message of purification.

Refinement

Welcome fires of refinement, and consider every trial to be an opportunity to advance in Me.

> *"My brethren, count it all joy when you fall into various trials, knowing that the testing of your faith produces patience. But let patience have its perfect work, that you may be perfect and complete, lacking nothing." (James 1:2-4 NKJV)*

If you live, as many do, avoiding trials along with pain, you will not become perfected. I want to test you, My beloved children, and if you will rely on Me completely, you will pass each test and advance to the next stage on your journey through the fire of refinement.

Gold

Gold is more valuable the purer it becomes. Pure gold can be poured as liquid, but those who are stubborn are not easily molded. I want my perfected, purified, believers to pour out their lives for the sake of the cross. Let Me shape you together to build bricks that fit perfectly together. The walls I put up are not to keep you in, but to send you from and to keep the Enemy out. Enter My Holy place and be lifted high to gain the understanding that I am the perfector of the saints. Willingness to be poured out is the only way My temple is built. Imagine if the cold, hard, bricks of all shapes and sizes came together, not willing to change to fit My plans. Nothing could be built, and if it were, it could not stand in the fire or through the testing.

Rebellion

My Spirit does not listen to the voice of rebellion, which is as the spirit of witchcraft, but my Spirit responds to the pure heart of the Father who also sends the Son. Souls are precious to My heart; this is why I went to the cross to conquer death, hell, and the grave.

> *"Do not harden your hearts as in the rebellion, in the day of trial in the wilderness, where your fathers tested Me, tried Me, and saw My works forty years." (Hebrews 3:8-9 NKJV)*

The Harvest

I commission you to help Me gather the harvest, for it is great and I am still waiting for workers to commit to My plan everywhere and now.

> *"Then He said to them, 'The harvest truly is great, but the laborers are few; therefore pray the Lord of the harvest to send out laborers into His harvest.'" (Luke 10:2 NKJV)*

Will you, My beloved sheep, hear My voice and ask how you can contribute in service to be a part of what you can see is being prepared as a table before you? I have invited you to feast with an invitation, and though I have called you to come, many have said, "I'm not hungry" and remain in the past. The fire is burning and the food is here. Will you come?

The Bread of Life

Evangelism of the lost is what My purpose is, not just a show of signs and wonders. Find your place to function. Don't just wait to see if there is enough fire and food—become the fire and be the food as I Myself have said, "I am the Bread of Life—the Living Water—set to pour from this Rock on which I invite you to stand.

Yeshua is My name;

Evangelism by fire is NOT a game.

The time is short. Find your area of service, and do this as unto Me!

> *"I am the living bread which came down from heaven. If anyone eats of this bread, he will live forever; and the bread that I shall give is My flesh, which I shall give for the life of the world." (John 6:51 NKJV)*

December 2012

December 5 – Fantasy vs. Reality

Reality

The reality of My Kingdom is as concrete as what spoke granite together to form rock. The earth was null and void; therefore, what is made was made from the spoken Word of what always was. "Since the beginning" speaks of the beginning of planet Earth, not the beginning of Father, Son, and Holy Spirit. Nothing is that was not made. The reality is that the Kingdom—not what is seen but what is not seen—is more real than what you see.

> *"In the beginning God created the heavens and the earth. The earth was without form, and void; and darkness was on the face of the deep. And the Spirit of God was hovering over the face of the waters. Then God said, 'Let there be light'; and there was light...." (Genesis 1 NKJV)*

Every sickness and every disease must bow and confess that Jesus, the Son of Man, is Lord, who says and does only what I, the Father, say and do through the power of the Holy Spirit that is within you now.

Fantasy

Fantasy is at war against My reality, trying to imitate that which is real to become a discredit, causing an unholy exchange:

What is real for what is not;

  What is plastic and cheap for what is foundationally solid;

    Like a diamond that cuts through stone,

      Rock versus what is manmade, and

        Crushes under the Rock.

Why do so many settle for counterfeit?

  Lust versus love;

    Money that spends versus money that does not;

      Lies versus truth;

        Light versus darkness;

          Standard versus compromise;

        The cross versus a tree;

      Santa versus Christ; and

    Santa's elves versus God's angels.

  I AM is who sees you when you're sleeping.

I AM is who knows when you're awake.

The Christmas Tree

If you adore and adorn your Christmas tree as the pagans and worship it, allowing it to be the center focus of Christmas, this is idolatry.

> *"Thus says the Lord: 'Do not learn the way of the Gentiles; do not be dismayed at the signs of heaven, for the Gentiles are dismayed at them. For the customs of the peoples are futile; for one cuts a tree from the forest, the work of the hands of the workman with the ax. They decorate it with silver and gold; they fasten it with nails and hammers so that it will not topple. They are upright, like a palm tree, and they cannot speak; they must be carried, because they cannot go by themselves. Do not be afraid of them, for they cannot do evil, nor can they do any good.' Inasmuch as there is none like You, O Lord. You are great and Your name is great in might."* (Jeremiah 10:2-6 NKJV)

One

Worship the giver, not the gift. When you worship the Son, you also worship the Father, in spirit and truth. Be mindful, My children, that I, the Lord your God, am one, and oneness is what I've called you to.

> *"Hear, O Israel: The Lord our God, the Lord is one!"* (Deuteronomy 6:4 NKJV)

> *"And the glory which You gave Me I have given them, that they may be one just as We are one."* (John 17:22 NKJV)

Will you be as I have intended? Be mindful of the cross—not what has died, but what now lives, and you will also be made alive by My Spirit that now sets you free. The world is only the shell, but I offer you My seed to become duplicators of the reality of My Kingdom. My reality will always trump the fleeting ritual of religious practice that can fill nothing but man's ego. My Spirit is not a practice but the reality of all that lives. Come and receive!

Seek Wisdom

Fantasy beckons you to become enamored by her beauty, but she is an idol of ashes, smoke, and mirrors—an illusion of what is not, impersonating what is. Follow her and love her, and surely, you will die in hopelessness. Follow the reality of My promises and you will see dreams actualized as things that are made from faith. Their inventor is the great and mighty, unmatchless King of Kings and Lord of Lords, El Shaddai, Jesus Christ who saves. Do not block the door to your heart with fantasy's lustrous light show, but seek wisdom from heaven by writing My promises on your hearts so they become substance for your soul, both now and forevermore. Amen.

December 14 – Christmas

Liberation of the Cross

Christmas is My favorite celebration of the year. The heavens rejoice at the memories of baby Jesus developing in the limitations of the human condition. My church at large today is in need of a physician. What did the cross really accomplish if not total liberation? Many still emphasize self-effort, deceived into thinking they need to save themselves. I have given you the keys that unlock the doors of heaven, yet so many do not open the door, bound and imprisoned by misunderstanding My Word. Improper application of My Word brings sickness and disease.

Faith

Faith is in need of developing. It is a shield—not an arm patch or merit badge.

> *"Above all, taking the shield of faith with which you will be able to quench all the fiery darts of the wicked one."*
> *(Ephesians 6:16 NKJV)*

People who believe I want them to remain in suffering here on earth have simply misunderstood My plan to produce in them character, perseverance, and patience. You see, once this goal has been achieved, I can remove the Enemy's hand and victory can be obtained.

Love

I will bring you into a new understanding of My love. My love is made perfect in weakness.

> *"And He said to me, 'My grace is sufficient for you, for My strength is made perfect in weakness.' Therefore most gladly I will rather boast in my infirmities, that the power of Christ may rest upon me." (2 Corinthians 12:9 NKJV)*

This weakness is what brings the surrender, and once full surrender is achieved and faith from dependence replaces fear, I can lift your pain. Some say, "I'm meant to go through this and that" because they know I use trials to produce strength. However, to think you are not meant to be free and in victory is deception from the Enemy who would love to take you down and show all those watching that to be a Christian means suffering. No unbeliever would be attracted to this kind of hopelessness.

Joy

I want your joy to be full. Fullness of joy, released by My presence, brings freedom.

> *"You will show me the path of life; in Your presence is fullness of joy; at your right hand are pleasures forevermore." (Psalm 16:11 NKJV)*

Singing and shouting in victory through a triumphant life—this is what brings converts into life—not dead works that can produce nothing. My work is full of life or it is not My work. If My life is in you, then you will be a light and many will step from their darkness.

Religious Pride

"Religious Pride" is at the root of the mindset that says, "I need to help Jesus suffer." Jesus does not have need of your help, you who suffer from self-righteous piety! Vanity. It's all vanity! Did My finished work on the cross not accomplish anything? Do you not see this mindset only produces a sense of working hard to find yourself approved by what you do instead of what's already been done by Me?

A Baby Born to Die

Baby Jesus was born to die, and I want you, My people, to learn to die to the rote routine of your works from self-effort that achieve only hypocrisy, and live! "Having the life" means having Jesus fully manifest upon you. Do you think you have the life of Jesus fully manifest upon you? Do you struggle with hopelessness, depression, discouragement, or chronic fatigue? These are produced by trying to accomplish what could not be done apart from the finished work of the cross. Do you know that when you are made alive again into new life with Christ, it is no longer you who love but Christ in you, the hope of glory?

> *"The mystery which has been hidden from ages and from generations, but now has been revealed to His saints. To them God willed to make known what are the riches of the glory of this mystery among the Gentiles: which is Christ in you, the hope of glory. Him we preach, warning every man and teaching every man in all wisdom, that we may present every man perfect in Christ Jesus." (Colossians 1:26-28 NKJV)*

This is what it means to have been born again into new life. If you have received this message, it will produce joy, and

  Joy releases faith, and

    Faith crushes fear, and

      Fear, when crushed, cannot destroy you

        Or your body,

          Or the bodies of your family.

New life, born new, new wholeness, new mindset, and new understanding helps you stand under My promise instead of under the burden you were not meant to carry. The Enemy brought the burden to you—not your Savior who saves those who will allow it.

Lord of All

Press on toward the prize with joy set before you so you can receive that which was lost.

> *"I press toward the goal for the prize of the upward call of God in Christ Jesus." (Philippians 3:14 NKJV)*

Will you let Me be Lord of all? Will you know that:

  No matter how hard you work;

    No matter how hard you study;

      No matter how much you can quote from My words;

        You cannot justify yourself?

> *"Therefore we conclude that a man is justified by faith apart from the deeds of the law." (Romans 3:28 NKJV)*

So believe in My promises, and do not think that I, the Lord your God, would have left you to carry weights that sink you into the seas of despair. I have come to take your burden, saying that you now have been made strong. I free you now to do My work, free indeed as I light your path toward victory as a contagious, outrageous, bold conqueror who will not fail if you just believe. Do you deny Me My right to be Lord of all? Repent and receive.

Faith in Action

Effort misplaced is a waste of time. Many people do the work just so they can feel good about who they are, seeking My approval. But I have already approved of you, My child. So now be free, as I Myself am free so you do not teach others to be bound so they, too, will be attracted to freedom and victory, empowered by My Spirit to cast off the mindset of judgment from a critical spirit of accusation. And renew the mind inside your surrendered heart by My Spirit, and remember that by My stripes you are healed. Receive it—you who stand for the Law yet practice lawlessness by your lack of faith. Be faith-filled and faithful so I can approve of your faith as your finisher.

> *"Therefore we also, since we are surrounded by so great a cloud of witnesses, let us lay aside every weight, and the sin which so easily ensnares us, and let us run with endurance the race that is set before us, looking unto Jesus, the author and finisher of our faith, who for the joy that was set before Him endured the cross, despising the shame, and has sat down at the right hand of the throne of God." (Hebrews 12:1-3 NKJV)*

Faith in action starts with a thought. Think about it, then do as My Spirit leads, according to My will to make all things new.

> *"Then He who sat on the throne said, 'Behold, I make all things new.' And he said to me, 'Write, for these words are true and faithful.'" (Revelation 21:5 NKJV)*

Humble yourselves and I will lift you up.

> *"Humble yourselves in the sight of the Lord, and He will lift you up." (James 4:10 NKJV)*

My will is firm that you might live a life of abundance, both here and now.

> *"The thief does not come except to steal, and to kill, and to destroy. I have come that they may have life, and that they may have it more abundantly." (John 10:10 NKJV)*

Appendix

The following testimonials, or stories, took place after the time frame of the journal entries recorded in this book. They have been randomly selected and names have been withheld or changed to uphold privacy.

"And they overcame him by the blood of the Lamb and by the word of their testimony." (Revelation 12:11a NKJV)

Testimony: Watches

I love watches!

I purchased a beautiful black and silver Invicta watch. At a house party, the Lord says to me, "Take off your watch and give it to that fellow over there." I did. The fellow responds by saying, "Did you know it's my birthday?" I say, "No, but God did!"

Later, I was given a second watch, and I gave it to someone the Lord designated. When He gave me a third watch, I gave it to the lot attendant at the Subaru dealership. Yes, another watch, number four, black and gold, was given to me and it, too, I gave away. Now the Lord gave me the nicest watch of all, worth $4,000, and by His prompting, I released the fifth one as well. The sixth watch was a red and silver, custom bolt, Invicta, and you guessed it—I gave it away. The next two watches, seven and eight, I gave to two pastors. The day I released the last watch, I was given a travel trailer I had asked the Lord for.

Watch number nine was a white Kenneth Cole and I gave it to a coworker. I tried to buy one online to replace it, but the Lord stopped me by saying, "I will replace the one you gave away." So, He did. Number ten was a beautiful black and gold, Invicta, Pro-Diver with mother-of-pearl inside with three circles reminding me of the Father, Son, and Holy Spirit. I gave that one to a pastor, of course. Forty-eight hours later, I received the eleventh watch, the same make and style except much bigger with a propeller inside the back. I gave that to a friend of mine who, in return, gave me a Gold Wing motorcycle. Watch number twelve was given to me on August 26, 2012, and it was solar-powered by light. Five minutes after I received it, obeying the Lord's prompting, I gave it away.

> *"Give, and it will be given to you: good measure, pressed down, shaken together, and running over will be put into your bosom. For with the same measure that you use, it will be measured back to you." (Luke 6:38 NKJV)*

These incidents took place nine years ago. I can't tell you how many watches I have received and given away since then…one just last week!

Testimony: Metal Dissolved

While I was ministering in Alberta, Canada, I heard the Lord say He was going to dissolve metal. As the Lord highlighted a certain woman, I pointed in her direction and said, "Right over there, raise your hand if it's you!" She raised her hand and I began to speak the words God was giving me for her. "The Lord is dissolving the metal in your body so that you will no longer set off the metal detectors at the airport. You are being healed in Jesus' name!"

She felt something happening in her body as she was deeply touched by the Holy Spirit. I shared that the Lord had not forgotten her and that she was made in His image and likeness to shine and be a witness for Him.

A few weeks later, I heard a report that she was completely healed. She is no longer setting off metal detectors! She also decided, as a result of God's goodness, she would no longer live the lifestyle of a lesbian. She was delivered from her anger against God and is now following Jesus. Remember, it is His goodness that leads a person to repentance, not our judgment to call people out.

> *"And do you think this, O man, you who judge those practicing such things, and doing the same, that you will escape the judgment of God? Or do you despise the riches of His*

> *goodness, forbearance, and longsuffering, not knowing that the goodness of God leads you to repentance?" (Romans 2:3-4 NKJV)*

The Lord, as the righteous judge, does not condemn us; rather He judges to evaluate with a heart to restore.

> *"Beloved, if our heart does not condemn us, we have confidence toward God." (1 John 3:21 NKJV)*

I see so many people who repent because of this Gospel. Gospel still means good news. It's only news if we proclaim it. Always be ready to give an account for the hope that is in you.

> *"But sanctify the Lord God in your hearts, and always be ready to give a defense to everyone who asks you a reason for the hope that is in you, with meekness and fear." (1 Peter 3:15 NKJV)*

Testimony: My First Boat

I asked the Lord for a boat. He said to call Mickey. The only Mickey I knew was an old neighborhood friend I hadn't talked to in many years. I called him and said, "Hey, Mickey, how are you?"

"Doing okay," he said.

"Are you selling a boat?"

"I'm going to be selling one. How did you know?"

"What is it?"

"Mickey responded, "It's a thirty-two-foot Carver."

"Can I come see it?"

"Sure, come on over."

When I saw it, I wondered if I would be able to drive such a large boat because I had never owned a boat before. I also didn't have the money to buy such a boat, but I knew the Lord could provide the money. After Mick told me the price, I told him I would see what I could do.

The Lord said, "Go get a slip." I responded by telling Him I didn't have the money to buy the boat, so why should I get a slip to store a boat I don't have and can't afford to buy? But, obediently, I called down to the Gig Harbor Marina and asked if they had any slips available for a thirty-two-foot boat. They said no! They were full up with forty-plus people on a waiting list and told me to try again next year. I asked them if they could put my name on a list. They said, "Sure."

Later, that same day, the Marina called and said a slip had opened up. This had God's signature all over it! I went down to the dock to locate the slip. It was all the way out on the end of the dock, a perfect place for a beginner to moor a boat easily. I said I would take it and signed my name to the contract, agreeing to pay the monthly moorage fee for the boat I didn't have.

Soon after stepping out in faith, the money came. Now I was the proud owner of a beautiful cruiser with a galley, mess, two heads, and it could sleep six. I used it as a waterfront office and place of prayer when I wasn't taking guests sightseeing on the waters of Puget Sound. Two big 350 cruiser engines made getting around very easy, and the memories will be with us forever.

After enjoying the cruiser for several years, we sold it for the same amount we had paid. Since then, we have sowed (given away) boats and received boats. It's always an incredible thing to see the Lord reward our faith and bring increase. He said that you reap what you sow, meaning the same type of substance. When I give watches away, I receive watches in return. When I give vehicles away, I receive vehicles; giving suits, I receive suits; releasing boats, I receive boats!

> *"Do not be deceived, God is not mocked; for whatever a man sows, that he will also reap." (Galatians 6:7 NKJV)*

Testimony: Another Boat

I asked the Lord for another boat, a smaller one, easy to maneuver—one I could take out of the water to avoid paying moorage fees—a fun boat to play with in the summer months.

While visiting a friend, I noticed he had a Tige, a competition ski boat—a model I had loved as a young water-skier. I asked him about it and he said, "Do you want it?"

"I would love it!" I responded.

"It's yours," he said.

Wow, was I ever excited! This boat just needed a bit of love and care. I spent most of the summer fixing it up: washing and waxing it, changing the oil; giving it new plugs, wires, cap rotor, and carpet; painting the trailer; adding new decals; and buffing out the wheels. You get the idea.

I could hardly wait to test it! The Lord even told me what lake to go to. Since we also had close friends living on the same lake, I invited one of them to come along. He agreed to meet me at the public dock, and we took it for my first run. I was so impressed with how it handled and how much power that 350 motor put out. I told my friend how I got the boat.

With some amazement, he said, "Someone just gave you this?"

"Yup! It's just exactly what I asked the Lord for."

He countered, "Well, usually when someone gives a boat away, it's not very nice, but this one is really nice."

Right then, the Lord said, "Give him the boat." What? I didn't say anything right away. At home, I told my wife how awesome our new boat performed, adding how I felt the Lord was asking me to give it to our friends. To my surprise, she readily agreed. "They will love it!" she quipped.

Later, these same friends invited us to dinner at their beautiful lakefront home, so we hooked up the boat. As we drove up the driveway, they came out to greet us, surprised to see the boat being towed. "Why did you bring the boat? Are we going skiing? It's kind of cold!"

I said, "The boat is for you!"

"No, you're not giving me that boat!"

"Yes I am."

He said, "No you aren't!" It was hard for him to believe. He said, "Do you know what day it is? I didn't know what he was referring to. "It's my birthday." I replied, "I didn't know it, but God did." Talk about blowing him away! The Lord knew that cruising the lake was one of this couple's favorite things to do. It had been a couple of years since they had sold their previous boat. Now they could again enjoy cruising the waterways of their lakefront neighborhood.

The Lord gives good gifts. He also loves to answer our prayers. Whatever you are believing for—a restored marriage, job improvement, healing, or the return of a prodigal child—the Lord loves to answer your prayers. Remember how the Scripture says that He hears us and answers us. He also says that we have not because we ask not. Anything we ask for in His name, *if* we believe, we will receive.

"If you ask anything in My name, I will do it." (John 14:14 NKJV)

"You fight and war. Yet you do not have because you do not ask." (James 4:2b NKJV)

"Therefore I say to you, whatever things you ask when you pray, believe that you receive them, and you will have them." (Mark 11:24 NKJV)

Testimony:
The Suburban and the Audi

After a struggling business owner's car was repossessed, I was asked if I could help by giving him a ride home. I said I would, so I drove over to pick him up in my Suburban and take him to his house. On the way, the Lord said to me, "Tell him how I gave you this Suburban."

I began to share with him how I had been asked to pray for a football player who tore his rotator cuff during a game. I happened to be watching the game at the time, so I made my way down to the playing field. After prayer, the young man was immediately healed, went right back into the game, and played harder than he had all season. Had he not been healed, he would have been out for the rest of the season. In gratitude, his dad gave me this Suburban.

He responded, "What? God just gave you this Suburban?"

"Yes, and he could do the same for you."

"Wow, I really needed to hear this story!"

Right then, I heard the Spirit of God say, "Give him your Suburban." I was not excited about that request in the moment because I had been elated when the Lord gave it to me in the first place. I had only had it for a short time, so I called my wife to see what she thought, part of me hoping she would say no.

"What will you drive?" she responded. I told her the Lord said he would repay me and I believed Him.

"Well, you'd better do it then!"

So, I got the title and drove over to this fellow's failing gym. I gave him the keys and title and said, "The Suburban is yours now." I had no idea he had asked the Lord for a Suburban with a Vortex V8 engine. He needed a seven-passenger vehicle for his family. It was fun seeing his face light up when he said, "No way!"

Thirty minutes later, one of the CEOs I had been serving told me to come to his office. He seemed oddly nervous as he told me that he had told God that if I gave my Suburban to his friend, he would give me his brand new A7 supercharged Audi. "I didn't think you would do it, but you did, so here's the keys and the title."

"What? Wow, are you sure? That is totally amazing because that's my wife's dream car!"

I gave it to Danielle and bought another Suburban. What an upgrade—that Audi was worth ten times as much as that Suburban. My wife is loving hearing and obeying God!

Testimony: Introduction to President Trump

In the past, I have asked the Lord to introduce me to certain high profile leaders—leaders like Joel Osteen and Joseph Prince—as a present on my birthday. He surprisingly answered this very specific prayer, right on the day of my birthday, which I had forgotten about. (I tell this story in my second book, *Rushing the Flood Gates of Heaven*.)

Knowing that He loves me, as He also loves you, and desires to give good gifts to those He loves, I asked Him again, "For my birthday this year, Lord, would you introduce me to President Trump and Melania?"

He said, "Yes, I'll set it up!"

Months later, I was asked by the Lord to go to Washington, DC for an event called, "The Return," a global movement of prayer and repentance, taking place on September 26, 2020. While there, I was in my hotel room when the Lord said, "Put on your shoes and go downstairs." I quickly responded. Once downstairs, I was led to go to the hotel diner. After being seated, a man I didn't know, sitting at the next table, said, "Hey, are you meeting someone?"

"No, I'm by myself."

"Would you join me for breakfast?"

I heard the Lord say, "Yes" so I did. While we were getting acquainted, and after I had prophesied over him, a woman from another table walked by me and I heard the Holy Spirit say, "Back pain, neck pain."

I said, "Ma'am, do you have neck and back pain?"

She stopped and said, "Yes, how did you know that?"

"Jesus lives in me. He knows everything, and He told me that He wants to heal you. Can I say a quick prayer for you?"

"Okay."

After asking and receiving permission to place my hand on her back where the pain was, I commanded it to leave and asked the Lord to heal that same area. Then I led her in a prayer to be filled with the Holy Spirit and to be baptized in passion and fire by the Holy Spirit. She was in tears.

Surprised, she said, "All the pain is gone!" She returned to her table and started telling the other women she was eating with about what had happened. One by one, they came over to our table asking for prayer. Some were healed and some were filled with the Holy Spirit.

> *"And Ananias went his way and entered the house; and laying his hands on him he said, 'Brother Saul, the Lord Jesus, who appeared to you on the road as you came, has sent me that you may receive your sight and be filled with the Holy Spirit.'" (Acts 9:17 NKJV)*

My new friend said, "This is amazing! Is a happening like this normal for you?"

I laughed as I said, "Yeah, it kind of is."

"Well, I'm a Baptist and I have never seen anything like this before."

He mentioned he was a congressman and shared that his daughter was an intern serving President Trump in the White House. He wanted to know if he could do anything for me. I told him I would love a personal tour of the White House. Right away, he called his daughter to make the arrangements and the available date was October 27, my birthday!

Three weeks later, I was back in DC.

The personal White House tour was amazing. I was even allowed to bring a few friends, and as we toured, we prayed over each office. President Trump and Melania had three or four campaign rallies that day, and before they left the White House, we were ushered out to watch them depart for West Salem, Wisconsin, on the Airforce One helicopter. As they neared the plane, the president, followed by Melania, turned around abruptly and headed straight toward me—me wearing my TRUMP mask! He fist-bumped me and we exchanged a few words. Among other things, I told him it was my birthday, that we loved him, and that he would win BIG! As he turned away to greet others, I was able to encourage Melania with words the Lord gave me.

Several news agencies caught the action. I think Fox was the first to show the video! Trump's personal photographer later phoned me and said she had snapped a shot of the fist-bump because it was unusual for the president to do that and asked if I would like a photo. Like one? I was so excited when a few days later I received the package of a beautifully embossed and padded presentation cover displaying the presidential seal and inside an 8 x 10 photo capturing the event—the day the Lord fulfilled my desire to meet the President of the United States, Donald J. Trump, on my birthday! *(Note: Perhaps it's significant to note that my birthday is a special time of celebration for me because just shy of thirty years ago and just before my birthday, I was in despair and attempted to take my life. I'm very much alive, and every October 27, I celebrate the goodness of God in saving me from death. (see "Nathan's Story" at the front of this book).*

I smile as I think about how precious it is to be a follower of Jesus. He knows our name and wants to give us the desires of our heart that He put there to reward.

> *"If you then, being evil, know how to give good gifts to your children, how much more will your Father who is in heaven give good things to those who ask Him!" (Matthew 7:11 NKJV)*

Addendum

Four Areas for Quick Reference: How to Hear My Voice; A Prayer to Receive Christ; A Prayer of Release; and A Prayer of Forgiveness of Self

How to Hear My Voice

I Will Teach You

I want you to teach others how to move in hearing My voice and how to exercise faith through prophecy. Prophecy is the result of hearing Me, for I tell you things you do not know. You have heard it said, "Don't show people how big your fish is—teach them how to fish." I am telling you to show others how to hear, just like you, yourself, have been hearing.

Steps to Hearing

1. Get quiet.

2. Communicate with God.

3. Expect to hear (getting your pen and paper ready is faith).

4. Write down what the Lord says.

5. Share with others as you are led by God.

Practicum

Many Christians hear different things about hearing My voice, but the truth about hearing is this: I am a rewarder of those who diligently seek Me.

> *"But without faith it is impossible to please Him: for he who comes to God must believe that He is, and that He is a rewarder of those who diligently seek Him." (Hebrews 11:6 NKJV)*

> *"My sheep hear My voice, and I know them, and they follow Me." (John 10:27 NKJV)*

I am the one who surrounds surrender. Faith is the substance of believing you will hear. Not believing you will hear is why people don't.

> *"Now faith is the substance of things hoped for, the evidence of things not seen." (Hebrews 11:1 NKJV)*

Say something like: "He (Jesus) is here right now," or "Adjust your awareness of His presence." Where two or more are gathered together, there I am in the midst of them.

> *"For where two or three are gathered together in My name, I am there in the midst of them." (Matthew 18:20 NKJV)*

Believe first and your faith will be fully manifest. Ask everyone to cry out to Me, "Jesus, are you there?" or "You are here, aren't you, Jesus? I am your built-in teacher!"

> *"A disciple is not above His teacher, but everyone who is perfectly trained will be like his teacher." (Luke 6:40 NKJV)*

A Prayer to Receive Christ

Lord God, I know I am a sinner. I believe You sent Your son, Jesus, to die on a cross for my sin. I repent of my wicked ways and ask You to come into my heart and fill me with Your Holy Spirit. Cleanse me of all unrighteousness and I will live for You from this day on. I want You to be my Lord. Thank You. Amen.

A Prayer of Release

Dear Lord: I choose to forgive _____ (name) for _____ (what they did) from my heart. I cancel all their debts and obligations to me. They owe me nothing! I ask you to forgive me for my bitterness and unforgiveness toward _____ (name) in this situation. In the name of Jesus and by the power of His blood, I cancel Satan's authority over me in this memory because I have forgiven _____ (name). I command all the tormentors assigned to me, because of my unforgiveness, to leave me now. Holy Spirit, I invite You into my heart to heal me of this pain. Please speak Your truth to me about this situation, and I will listen for your answer.

A Prayer of Forgiveness of Self

Dear Heavenly Father: In the name of Jesus, and as an act of my own free will, I confess, repent, and renounce my sin of _____ (specific sin of self-loathing). I ask you to forgive me for this sin. I choose to forgive myself for _____ (specific sin) from my heart. I release myself from any guilt and shame because of this self-bitterness. In the name of Jesus, and by the power of His blood, I cancel Satan's authority over me in this area because of my cooperation with self-bitterness. I command self-bitterness to go now. Holy Spirit, I invite you into my heart to heal me of self-bitterness. Please speak your words of truth to me about this situation, and I will listen quietly.

About the Author

Nathan Andrew French is the founder and leader of The Rock Revival Center located in Tacoma, Washington. He previously wrote *It's NOT Meant to Be a Secret: God wants to speak to you!* and *Rushing the Flood Gates of Heaven: For those who are thirsty!* Nathan is known in the Pacific Northwest and around the world as a prophetic evangelist, one who influences the nations for revival. He is a respected advisor to a number of corporate leaders and serves as a chaplain to various corporations. Nathan and his wife, Danielle, live with their two daughters in Gig Harbor, Washington.

Speaker Page

Nathan French Ministries

Nathan French Ministries

Nathan French Ministries represents Nathan's personal ministry and validates his willingness to respond to that still, small, voice of God—anywhere He leads. If you would like to contact Nathan with your ministry request, go to his website:

www.NathanFrenchMinistries.com

The Rock Revival Center

Nathan can be contacted online on The Rock Revival Center website: www.TheRockRevivalCenter.com and on Facebook at The Rock Revival Center. If you have questions about this revival ministry, send an email to:

info@rockrevivalcenter.com.

Awaken the Planet

Awaken the Planet is a revival hub and outreach ministry of The Rock Revival Center. Watch for upcoming events posted on the website:

www.AwakenThePlanet.com.

Also by Nathan A. French

If you enjoyed, ONE: *The Power of Unity!*, you will also enjoy Nathan's first book, *It's* NOT *Meant to Be a Secret: God wants to speak to you!* And his second book, *Rushing the Flood Gates of Heaven: For those who are thirsty.*

It's **NOT** *Meant to Be a Secret: God wants to speak to you!*

Have you ever wanted to hear the voice of God? Do you know that He wants to speak to you? Here in the pages of *It's* NOT *Meant to Be a Secret*, one man has dared to answer the call of Jeremiah 33:3: "Call to Me and I will answer you and show you great and mighty things which you do not know."

In the quiet of the night I heard Him say, "Come sit with Me." Jesus said, "It is I who purifies; it is I who redeems; it is I who delights in this moment you give to Me. I am honored to sit with you in My royal house."

Lord, what do You want me to do? The gate is open before you so I ask you to come; step into My presence as you have dared not in the past. Let the path I light up be your guide; let the signs along the way direct your going. Be not afraid for I am with you. As a friend, we will laugh together. I am that I am that I am that you follow—peace be with you, My child, whom I call friend.

Rushing the Flood Gates of Heaven: For those who are thirsty

In *Rushing the Flood Gates of Heaven: For those who are thirsty!*, author and pastor, Nathan French, brings a continuation of his first book, *It's NOT Meant to Be a Secret: God wants to speak to you!* This book, like the last, is a collection of powerful interchanges full of divine inspiration and instruction that will leave you riveted as you receive extraordinary secrets from heaven.

Nathan's daily journal entries record his conversations with God from September 2011 through April 2012. He shares again his dramatic story of drug abuse in his youth and how God worked a miracle to save his life. The son of a minister himself, Nathan then devoted his life to God, ultimately becoming the pastor of The Rock of the Harbor Church *(now Rock Revival Center)* in Gig Harbor, Washington.

Get ready to take a ride into the depths of heaven that will leave you electrified with awe and wonder at the power of God's love. Readers are sure to be lifted by this stunning collection of revelations. God speaks in a clear, gentle, plain-spoken voice, yet the passages abound with Scriptural correlations. Ultimately, while these words are God's personal conversation with Nathan, they will inspire you to spend time alone with God to develop your own personal relationship with your Creator.

To purchase a copy of

It's NOT Meant to Be a Secret: God wants to speak to you!

or

Rushing the Flood Gates of Heaven: For those who are thirsty!

visit Amazon.com

Made in the USA
Columbia, SC
18 February 2022